A Tale of Two Cities

This is a work of fiction. All of the characters, events, and organizations portrayed in this work are either products of the authors' imagination or used fictitiously.

A Tale Of Two Cities
Copyright © 2014 by Christopher M. Walsh

Based on the novel by Charles Dickens.

Cover by David Blixt

All rights reserved. No part of this book may be reproduced in any form by any electronic or mechanical means including photocopying, recording, or information storage and retrieval without permission in writing from the author.

ISBN-13: 978-0692366356
ISBN-10: 0692366350

For information about production rights, e-mail:
walsh.christopher@gmail.com

Published by Sordelet Ink

A Tale of Two Cities

A PLAY BY
CHRISTOPHER M. WALSH

ADAPTED FROM THE NOVEL BY
CHARLES DICKENS

Published by
Sordelet Ink

A Tale Of Two Cities received its world premiere at Lifeline Theatre in Chicago, IL in 2014. It was directed by Elise Kauzlaric; the assistant director was Spencer Ryan Diedrick; original music and sound design was by Andrew Hansen; violence design was by Matt Hawkins; costume design was by Elsa Hiltner; lighting design was by Diane D. Fairchild; scenic design was by Joe Schermoly; properties design was by Jesse Gaffney; the production manager was Benjamin W. Dawson; and the stage manager was Shelby Glasgow. The cast was as follows:

THE RESURRECTION MAN - John Henry Roberts
DOCTOR MANETTE/GASPARD - Sean Sinitski
MONSIEUR DEFARGE - Dan Granata
MADAME DEFARGE - Carolyn Klein
LUCIE MANETTE - Maggie Scrantom
MISS PROSS - Katie McLean Hainsworth
CHARLES DARNAY - Nicholas Bailey
JOHN BARSAD/MARQUIS ST. EVREMONDE - Chris Hainsworth
SYDNEY CARTON/JACQUES #1 - Josh Hambrock
SEAMSTRESS - Melissa Engle

Understudies - Jess Berry, Joe Bianco, Luke Daigle, Katherine Schwartz

The following credit must appear in all programs/playbills handed to audience members at performances of A Tale Of Two Cities:

A Tale Of Two Cities was originally produced by
Lifeline Theatre, Chicago, Illinois, and premiered there in 2014.

Cast of Characters

RESURRECTION MAN - The zeitgeist in human form, appearing as a variety of common folk

DOCTOR MANETTE - A French doctor, father of Lucie, and a former inmate of the Bastille.

MONSIEUR DEFARGE - A French wine shop owner and early Revolutionary

MADAME DEFARGE - A French wine shop proprietor and early Revolutionary

LUCIE MANETTE - An English woman of French descent

MISS PROSS - An English governess

CHARLES DARNAY - A French nobleman in self-imposed exile

JOHN BARSAD - An English spy with several aliases

SYDNEY CARTON - An English barrister and alcoholic

GASPARD - A French commoner

MARQUIS ST. EVREMONDE - An arrogant French nobleman; Charles Darnay's uncle

JACQUES #1 - A French Revolutionary, part of the Defarges' inner circle

SEAMSTRESS - A young French woman waiting to be executed

PALL BEARERS

A PRIEST

REVOLUTIONARIES

Setting

Multiple locations in and around London and Paris, in the years leading up to and during the French Revolution.

ACT I

Scene One

(Lights up on the RESURRECTION MAN. His clothes and manner indicate a man who is used to manual labor. His hands and boots are covered in dried mud. He speaks with a Cockney accent)

RESURRECTION MAN
"It was the best of times, it was the worst of times; it was the age of wisdom, it was the age of foolishness; it was the epoch of belief, it was the epoch of incredulity; it was the season of Light, it was the season of Darkness; it was the spring of hope, it was the winter of despair." *(To the audience)* It is the Year of Our Lord Seventeen Hundred and Eighty-Three, and in England and in France life is about to get very interesting indeed. The word of the day, the year, the century, is, "Revolution." The Treaty of Paris has just ended one, and watered the seeds of another. Nothing new, really. Revolution. A resurrection. "I am the resurrection and the life, saith the Lord. He that believeth in me, though he were

dead, yet shall he live, and whosoever liveth and believeth in me, shall never die." You may call me the Resurrection Man. A fancy title, certainly, but it's not a job I can recommend to the faint of heart. It's one of those jobs you folk would prefer not to know about, but you can't live without it. One day you'll thank me for it. Now where was I? Oh yes. Revolution. Resurrection. For example...

(Lights up on DOCTOR MANETTE, in a dimly lit workroom. He sits on a bench with his back to us. He works on a shoe)

RESURRECTION MAN
Doctor Alexandre Manette, who is about to be recalled to life, here, during the best and worst of times.

(MONSIEUR DEFARGE and MADAME DEFARGE enter. MADAME DEFARGE carries knitting with her. She spends the whole scene standing back, knitting and observing)

MONSIEUR DEFARGE
Anything to report, Jacques?

RESURRECTION MAN
(With a French accent) Nothing at all, Jacques.

MONSIEUR DEFARGE
Send them in, and wait for us downstairs, Jacques.

RESURRECTION MAN
Yes, Jacques. *(To audience, back to his Cockney accent)* Oh, right. We're starting the story in France. My name isn't Jacques. Neither is his, for that matter. Those two would be Monsieur and Madame Defarge. This is their wine shop, in the

district of Paris known as Saint Antoine.

(The RESURRECTION MAN exits. LUCIE and MISS PROSS enter)

MONSIEUR DEFARGE
(To LUCIE and MISS PROSS) I must ask you to wait a moment. He was imprisoned in the Bastille for eighteen years. A shock like this must be delivered delicately.

MISS PROSS
We understand, Monsieur Defarge. You explained it all in your letter.

MONSIEUR DEFARGE
I did, Miss Pross, but I want to remind you once again. It is for your sake as much as his. Observing a man in his condition can be most upsetting.

(MISS PROSS looks to LUCIE, who nods her consent. MONSIEUR DEFARGE approaches DOCTOR MANETTE)

MONSIEUR DEFARGE
Good day!

DOCTOR MANETTE
(Pausing his work) Good day.

MONSIEUR DEFARGE
You are still hard at work, I see?

DOCTOR MANETTE
Yes... I am working. *(DOCTOR MANETTE's voice is distant: "the faintness of solitude and disuse.")*

MONSIEUR DEFARGE
Are you going to finish that pair of shoes today?

DOCTOR MANETTE
What did you say?

MONSIEUR DEFARGE
Do you mean to finish that pair of shoes today?

DOCTOR MANETTE
I can't say that I mean to. I suppose so. I don't know. *(Distracted, DOCTOR MANETTE resumes stitching the shoe)*

MONSIEUR DEFARGE
You have a visitor, you see.

DOCTOR MANETTE
What did you say?

MONSIEUR DEFARGE
Here is a visitor. *(MONSIEUR DEFARGE waves for Lucie to come forward. To DOCTOR MANETTE)* Come! Here is a young lady, who knows a well made shoe when she sees one. Show her that shoe you are working at. Take it, mademoiselle. *(DOCTOR MANETTE holds the shoe up submissively. LUCIE takes it)* Tell the young lady what kind of shoe it is, and the maker's name.

(Pause)

DOCTOR MANETTE
I forget what it was you asked me. What did you say?

MONSIEUR DEFARGE
I said, couldn't you describe the kind of shoe, for mademoiselle's information?

DOCTOR MANETTE
It is a lady's shoe. It is a young lady's walking shoe.

MONSIEUR DEFARGE
And the maker's name?

(Pause)

DOCTOR MANETTE
Did you ask for my name?

MONSIEUR DEFARGE
Assuredly I did.

DOCTOR MANETTE
One Hundred and Five, North Tower.

MONSIEUR DEFARGE
Is that all?

DOCTOR MANETTE
One Hundred and Five, North Tower.

MONSIEUR DEFARGE
Are you not a shoemaker by trade?

DOCTOR MANETTE
No. I... I learned it here. I asked leave to teach myself, and I got it with much difficulty after a long while, and I have made shoes ever since. *(DOCTOR MANETTE holds his hand out for the shoe. After a moment, LUCIE holds it out for him. DOCTOR MANETTE takes the shoe, then notices her hand)* What is this? *(He puts the shoe down and takes LUCIE's hand, examining it all over)* You are not the gaoler's daughter. Who are you? *(LUCIE sits down on the bench next to DOCTOR MANETTE. He continues examining her hand, then her face, then her hair)* It is the same. *(He runs his fingers through LUCIE's hair)* My wife... she laid her head upon my shoulder, that night when I was summoned. She had a fear

of my going, though I had none. And when I was brought to the North Tower they found strands of her hair upon my sleeve. I asked that they leave them. "They can never help me to escape in the body, though they may in the spirit." Those were the words I said. I remember them very well. *(He takes LUCIE's face in his hands)* How can this be?

(MISS PROSS and MONSIEUR DEFARGE step forward, but LUCIE waves them off)

LUCIE
I entreat you, do not come near us!

DOCTOR MANETTE
Whose voice was that? *(DOCTOR MANETTE lets LUCIE go and staggers backward)* No, no, no. You are too young. It can't be. Look at me. *(He holds up his hands)* These are not the hands she knew. This is not the face she knew. This is not a voice she ever heard. It was so long ago. Before the North Tower. Ages ago. *(He forces himself to calm down. He steps closer to LUCIE)* What is your name?

(LUCIE takes his hand)

LUCIE
Sir, if you hear in my voice any resemblance to one that once was sweet music in your ears; if in touching my hair you recall a beloved head that lay upon your shoulder when you were young and free; if I bring back the remembrance of a home long desolate while your poor heart pined away... Sir, my mother never spoke of my father. I never knew of the tortures he suffered. She hid them from me. Never have I striven all day and lain

awake and wept all night for his sake, and because of that I must ask his pardon. My name is Lucie, sir... do you know me now?

DOCTOR MANETTE
Are you... Are you my daughter?

LUCIE
Yes, father. It's me.

(They embrace. MISS PROSS and MONSIEUR DEFARGE step aside)

MISS PROSS
How is it he came to be in your care, Monsieur?

MONSIEUR DEFARGE
I worked for him, and his wife, many years ago. It was I who helped Madame Manette and the infant Lucie escape to England, once it was clear the Doctor would not be returning from the Bastille.

MISS PROSS
Is Doctor Manette fit for the journey?

MONSIEUR DEFARGE
More fit for the journey than to stay here, I think. Doctor Manette is, for all reasons, best out of France.

LUCIE
Come, Father. It's time for us to go home.

(DOCTOR MANETTE packs his tools and materials and allows LUCIE to lead him out. MISS PROSS follows. MADAME DEFARGE stops knitting and looks up at MONSIEUR DEFARGE. He shrugs apologetically. MISS PROSS, MONSIEUR DEFARGE, and MADAME DEFARGE exit)

Scene Two

(The RESURRECTION MAN enters as the scene shifts to a courtroom in London. During the shift, we see DOCTOR MANETTE transform from the broken prisoner of the first scene into the healthy retired gentlemen he has spent the last five years becoming. DOCTOR MANETTE and LUCIE take seats in the gallery)

RESURRECTION MAN
(Cockney accent) Five years pass, and in that time we see dear old Doctor Manette regain some semblance of his former self under the gentle care of Lucie, his daughter, and the ever-vigilant governess Miss Pross. Today, both father and daughter have been called upon, regarding an incident that occurred during their flight from France five years gone. On their crossing they made the acquaintance of this fellow...

(CHARLES DARNAY enters, and takes his place in the dock)

RESURRECTION MAN
One Charles Darnay, now in the dock on the charge of High Treason. Enter one Sydney Carton, counsel for the defense.

(CARTON enters, dressed in the robe and wig of a lawyer. The RESURRECTION MAN takes a moment looking back and forth between the two)

RESURRECTION MAN
Hard to imagine two men more different, one from the other, really. It is here, on this day, that their fates and the Manettes' are intertwined. Observe them close, for if this story belongs to anyone, it belongs to them. How the jury did sigh as lovely Miss Lucie provided her own recollection of the crossing, and of Mister Darnay.

LUCIE
(testifying) There were no other passengers that night, but we four. When Mister Darnay came on board, he noticed that my father was much fatigued and in a very weak state of health. He was so good as to advise me how I could shelter my father from the wind and weather. He expressed great gentleness and kindness for my father's state, and I am sure he felt it. He was as open in his confidence with me as he was kind, and good, and useful to me and to my father.

RESURRECTION MAN
Darnay is holding up well, don't you think? Especially when you consider that if he's found guilty then it's off to Tyburn to be hanged, drawn and quartered. We'll keep doing that for another ninety years. Civilized age that we live in. Mister Darnay stands accused by that fellow...

(BARSAD enters and sits in the witness box)

RESURRECTION MAN
John Barsad, gentleman, and unimpeachable patriot. At least that's what the prosecutors would have us think.

CARTON
Mister Barsad, in your testimony you stated that you witnessed the prisoner, Charles Darnay, embark upon the ferry at Calais where he met and exchanged documents with another man, also French by his language. Is that correct?

BARSAD
Indeed it is.

CARTON
And you have stated that you overheard conversation between the prisoner and this mysterious Frenchman that you found suspicious.

BARSAD
Indeed I did.

CARTON
You suspected the prisoner of colluding with enemies of England, specifically the former colonies of America, correct? Why?

BARSAD
I overheard a mention of George Washington.

CARTON
Of course. Mister Barsad, Lucie Manette has testified that she has no recollection of ever seeing you on the crossing from Calais to Dover. In fact, she stated that there were but four passengers on that crossing, and further, she has never seen your

face before today. How do you answer to that?

BARSAD
With all due respect, the young lady must be mistaken.

CARTON
I see. Have you ever been a spy, yourself?

BARSAD
No. I scorn the base insinuation.

CARTON
Ever been in prison?

BARSAD
Certainly not.

CARTON
Never in a debtors' prison?

BARSAD
I don't see what that's got to do with--

CARTON
Never in a debtors' prison? Come, once again. Never?

BARSAD
Yes.

CARTON
How many times?

BARSAD
Two or three times.

CARTON
Not five or six?

BARSAD
Perhaps.

CARTON
Ever been kicked?

BARSAD
Might have been.

CARTON
Frequently?

BARSAD
No.

CARTON
Ever kicked down the stairs?

BARSAD
Decidedly not. *(Pause)* Once I received a kick on the top of a staircase, but I fell down of my own accord.

CARTON
On that occasion, were you not kicked for cheating at dice?

BARSAD
Something to that effect was said by the intoxicated liar who committed the assault, but it was not true.

CARTON
You swear it was not true?

BARSAD
Positively.

CARTON
Ever live by cheating at games?

BARSAD
Never.

CARTON
Ever live by gambling?

BARSAD
Not more than any other gentleman.

CARTON
Do you have any expectation of profit from the evidence you have given today?

BARSAD
(Slight pause) No.

CARTON
You are not in regular government pay and employment?

BARSAD
Oh dear no.

CARTON
You swear to that?

BARSAD
Over and over again.

CARTON
No motives but those of sheer patriotism?

BARSAD
None whatsoever.

CARTON
Did you ever see the prisoner on any other occasion?

BARSAD
I did not.

CARTON
And yet you say you are quite sure that it was the

prisoner that you saw five years ago?

BARSAD
Quite sure.

CARTON
Did you ever see anybody very like the prisoner?

BARSAD
Not so alike that I could be mistaken.

(CARTON takes off his wig)

CARTON
Mister Barsad, look upon my face, if you would. Thank you. Now look upon the prisoner. How say you? Are we not very like each other?

(Whispers from the gallery. We hear the sound of the judge's gavel the court back to order)

CARTON
Mister Barsad?

BARSAD
You are rather alike, I suppose.

CARTON
Your solemn oath, sir: Can you claim that if you met one of us on the street, would you know which one of us you had met?

BARSAD
I can't say, sir.

CARTON
And yet you would have us believe that you can identify the prisoner as the same man you supposedly saw exchange documents with a still unidentified Frenchman, once, at night, five years ago? Or should we line up every poor fellow who

fits this vague description and try him for High Treason until we find our man? I have no further questions. Thank you, Mister Barsad.

(BARSAD exits)

RESURRECTION MAN
(To audience) I'll save you the suspense and let you know that our hero Charles Darnay was acquitted. Mister Barsad's rather embarrassing performance played no small role in the decision, but all agreed it was the testimony of Miss Lucie Manette that most swayed the jury's favor.

(The sound of the judge's gavel signals the end of the trial. CARTON and the RESURRECTION MAN exit. DARNAY steps out of the dock. LUCIE rushes up to congratulate him)

LUCIE
Mister Darnay?

DARNAY
Miss Manette?

LUCIE
It's very good to see you again, and out of harm's way.

DARNAY
I appreciated your kind words in your testimony. Thank you.

LUCIE
My father was very ill when we came here from France, and you were very kind to us on that crossing.

DARNAY
Good Doctor Manette, I'm glad to see you again,

and in much better health than when last we met.

(DARNAY holds his hand out to DOCTOR MANETTE, who just stares at him)

DOCTOR MANETTE
Have we… have we met before, Mister Darnay?

DARNAY
You were indisposed when we shared the ferry from Calais five years ago.

DOCTOR MANETTE
Still, there is a resemblance…

DARNAY
Yes, well, it seems I share a resemblance with a number of people today.

LUCIE
Father?

(DOCTOR MANETTE slowly turns to LUCIE)

LUCIE
Shall we go home?

(After an awkward moment, DOCTOR MANETTE seems to recall himself)

DOCTOR MANETTE
Forgive me. It was an infamous prosecution. I am glad you have been brought off with honor.

LUCIE
(To DARNAY) Bless you, sir. I hope you have been preserved this day for a prosperous and happy life. Good day!

(LUCIE and DOCTOR MANETTE exit. CARTON enters and sees DARNAY staring off

after LUCIE)

CARTON
That's a fair young lady to be pitied by, and wept for by.

DARNAY
Oh! Mister Carton, forgive me. I have not properly thanked you for all you did for me today.

(CARTON goes to pack up his paperwork)

CARTON
I have done my best for you, Mister Darnay, and my best is as good as another man's.

DARNAY
Much better, I say. To think my future hinged on a passing resemblance... Are we really so alike, do you think?

CARTON
Like enough for Mister Barsad.

DARNAY
Still, I should like to show you some token of gratitude. Have you dined?

CARTON
I have, during the deliberations. Good night.

(CARTON finishes packing the last of his paperwork and starts to exit)

DARNAY
Well you can at least let me buy you drink.

CARTON
This way, then.

Scene Three

(The scene shifts to a pub. The RESURRECTION MAN enters wearing an apron and serves drinks as DARNAY and CARTON sit across from each other. CARTON drinks heavily)

DARNAY
I hardly seem to belong to this world again.

CARTON
I don't wonder at it. It's not so long since you were pretty far on your way to another. *(CARTON pours a drink for DARNAY who takes it, but does not drink right away)* As for me, the greatest desire I have is to forget I belong to the world at all. It has no good in it for me, nor I for it. So we are not much alike in that particular. Indeed, I begin to think we are not much alike in any particular, you and I. *(CARTON takes a drink)* Funny thing about that Barsad fellow.

DARNAY
Yes.

CARTON
No. I mean, I suppose it was funny, making a hash of his testimony the way he did. But that's not what I'm talking about.

DARNAY
No?

CARTON
No. I've dealt with his type before. I would not be surprised to learn that "John Barsad" is not even his real name. He's a rat by nature. He traffics in information, and he does nothing for free.

DARNAY
What exactly are you saying, Mister Carton?

CARTON
Why were you making the crossing that night, five years ago?

DARNAY
I had promise of employment. I am a tutor in French language and literature.

CARTON
That's where you were headed. I'm wondering from where you came.

DARNAY
My family is from--

CARTON
From Paris, yes. And "Darnay" is in fact an Anglicized pronunciation of the family name, "D'Aulnais."

DARNAY
That is correct.

CARTON
Your mother's family's name.

DARNAY
I must ask, why this sudden interest in my history before coming to England?

CARTON
My own edification. But what you should ask is, who would pay John Barsad to perjure himself by claiming to have followed you across the Channel, and then falsely accuse you of being a spy?

DARNAY
I'm sure I don't know what you mean.

CARTON
Someone went to some expense to have you removed from the world. You don't wish to tell me, well, the case is finished and our business is done. *(CARTON raises his glass)* Now why don't you give a toast, Mr. Darnay?

DARNAY
What toast, do you think?

CARTON
It's on the tip of your tongue, I'm certain.

DARNAY
To Miss Manette.

CARTON
Miss Manette, then. *(They drink)* How does it feel?

DARNAY
What do you mean?

CARTON
Is it worth being tried for one's life, to be the object of such sympathy and compassion? *(DARNAY does not answer)* Let me ask you another question. Do you think I particularly like you?

DARNAY
Really, Mister Carton, I have not asked myself the question.

CARTON
Ask it now.

DARNAY
You have acted as if you do... But no, I don't think you do.

CARTON
I don't think I do, either.

DARNAY
I hope that will not prevent you from accepting my thanks, in any case.

CARTON
I neither want thanks nor merit any. It was nothing to do, in the first place, and in the second, you were my client. What did you expect me to do? You wish to thank me? Then have them bring me another bottle.

(Not knowing how to answer, DARNAY stands up to leave)

DARNAY
Farewell, Mister Carton.

CARTON
Do you think I am drunk?

DARNAY
I think you have been drinking.

CARTON
You know I have been drinking.

DARNAY
I do know it. And I do think you are drunk.

CARTON
I care for no man on earth, Mister Darnay, and no man on earth cares for me.

DARNAY
Much to be regretted.

CARTON
Maybe so. Maybe not.

DARNAY
Good night, Mister Carton.

(DARNAY exits. The RESURRECTION MAN enters, still wearing the apron, cleaning up the pub)

CARTON
Do I particularly like the man?

RESURRECTION MAN
Sorry, sir?

CARTON
Why should I, just because he resembles me? There is nothing in me to like.

RESURRECTION MAN
Oh, I don't know that, sir.

CARTON
Oh, what a fine reason for taking to a man. He shows you what you have fallen away from. He

shows you what you might have been. Were I to change places with him, would that lovely girl have looked on me in the same way? I shall say it in plain words. I hate the fellow.

(CARTON examines his reflection in his glass. After a moment, he takes the bottle with him as he exits)

Scene Four

(The scene shifts to DOCTOR MANETTE's bedroom. DOCTOR MANETTE is sleepwalking. He is dressed for bed. He paces back and forth, agitated. The RESURRECTION MAN observes him)

DOCTOR MANETTE
They have no part in His mercies. They and their descendants, to the last of their race, I denounce to the times when all these things shall be answered for. I denounce them to Heaven and to earth. *(DOCTOR MANETTE continues to pace)*

RESURRECTION MAN
In the dead of night he walks in his room, back and forth, back and forth. The Doctor's mind at these times is still walking in his old prison cell.

(LUCIE enters. DOCTOR MANETTE does not notice her. She takes his hand and paces with him)

RESURRECTION MAN
Miss Lucie has learned that these spells come at times of great agitation, when the Doctor has seen something, or someone, that recalls to him his frightful past. She'll go to him then, saying not a word, and walk with him until he is composed again.

(LUCIE and DOCTOR MANETTE exit)

Scene Five

(The scene shifts to the home of the MARQUIS ST. EVREMONDE. The RESURRECTION MAN removes his apron, and replaces it with the livery of the MARQUIS' servants)

RESURRECTION MAN
Let us turn our attention south, across the Channel, to a village with its one poor street, with its poor brewery, poor tannery, poor tavern, poor stable-yard, poor fountain, all usual poor appointments. It had its poor people too. According to solemn inscription in the little village, the tax for the state, the tax for the church, the tax for the lord, tax local and tax general, were to be paid here and to be paid there, until the wonder was, that there was any village left unswallowed. Overlooking this poor domain - one of the many found in France - is the estate of the Marquis St. Evremonde. Today I am one Thomas Gabelle, humble servant, beneath the notice of the Monseigneur.

(The MARQUIS enters)

MARQUIS
How long has she been waiting?

RESURRECTION MAN
(French accent) Several hours now, Monseigneur. She was most agitated when she arrived.

MARQUIS
What is she? A seamstress, you said? Well, she has hung on the vine long enough, I think. Send her in.

RESURRECTION MAN
Very good, Monsieur the Marquis.

(The RESURRECTION MAN goes to the doorway and signals. The SEAMSTRESS enters. The RESURRECTION MAN exits, leaving her alone with the MARQUIS. Unsure what to do next, she drops to a low curtsey)

SEAMSTRESS
Monsieur the Marquis.

MARQUIS
Madame.

SEAMSTRESS
Monsieur, I have come... I have come... It's my husband, Monsieur.

MARQUIS
What of him?

SEAMSTRESS
I have come to beg for your leniency.

MARQUIS
I see. Why do you believe I have any power to influence his fate?

SEAMSTRESS
Because it is by your will he is imprisoned.

MARQUIS
Madame, have you not heard the charges leveled against your husband?

SEAMSTRESS
He was drunk, Monsieur. He was just talking.

MARQUIS
Just talking. Did you hear what he said, while he was "just talking?"

SEAMSTRESS
I was not there.

MARQUIS
A shame. Perhaps you could have had a restraining influence upon him. Instead it falls to me to maintain order.

SEAMSTRESS
He spoke no treason--

MARQUIS
He spread lies and dissent. He spoke out against the aristocracy. He set himself in opposition to the noble families that rightly govern this land. He wished to sew the seeds of discord and rebellion.

SEAMSTRESS
No, Monsieur! How could he? He's just a shopkeeper.

MARQUIS
Perhaps. Perhaps he was simply drunk, as you say. But can I take that chance? How can I maintain order if I allow such slander to go unpunished? *(Pause)* I have your assurance that your husband

will remain silent from now on?

SEAMSTRESS
Oh yes, Monsieur. You have my word.

MARQUIS
That is well. But I believe I will need something more.

SEAMSTRESS
More? Monsieur, I don't know anything. I wasn't there. I don't know who was there. I had never set foot in that wine shop before--

MARQUIS
You misunderstand me. You are a young woman, and not unattractive, considering. What do you think I want?

SEAMSTRESS
But--

MARQUIS
I don't have to ask.

(Pause)

SEAMSTRESS
If I do this, do you promise to free my husband?

MARQUIS
I promise that you shall never see him again if you do not.

SEAMSTRESS
You leave me no choice, Monsieur.

MARQUIS
There is always a choice, Madame.

(After a beat, the SEAMSTRESS nods)

MARQUIS
See that we are not interrupted.

RESURRECTION MAN
Yes, Monsieur. *(The MARQUIS exits. The RESURRECTION MAN switches back to Cockney)* Beneath it all, hidden in the hearts of the downtrodden, an ember smolders, waiting to be stoked into a roaring flame. It is beneath the dignity of the Marquis to notice it, but it will not be long now before the whole country burns.

(The SEAMSTRESS exits slowly. The RESURRECTION MAN removes the trappings of the MARQUIS' home, transitioning back to the MANETTES)

Scene Six

(We hear a low rumble of thunder as the scene shifts to the home of LUCIE MANETTE and her father. The shoemaker's workbench stands in a corner. DARNAY enters)

DARNAY
Miss Manette? Doctor? *(Finding himself alone, DARNAY looks around. MISS PROSS enters and finds him looking at the shoemaker's bench)* I wonder what this is here for?

MISS PROSS
And why wonder at that?

DARNAY
Oh! Miss Pross, lovely to see you again. *(She just stares at him)* I'm sorry, the maid said that Doctor and Miss Manette were home and that I should come in. I should have thought--

MISS PROSS
You should have! How do you do, Mister Darnay?

DARNAY
Uh, pretty well, thank you... How are you?

MISS PROSS
I am very much put out.

DARNAY
I see. May I ask why?

MISS PROSS
I don't want dozens of people who are not at all worthy to come here looking after Miss Lucie.

DARNAY
Do dozens come here for that purpose?

MISS PROSS
Hundreds.

DARNAY
Dear me.

MISS PROSS
I have lived with the darling girl - or she has lived with me - since she was ten years old. And it's really very hard. All sorts of people who are not in the least degree worthy, always turning up. It was hard enough when Doctor Manette came, not that I find any fault with Doctor Manette, except that he is not worthy of such a daughter, but that's nothing against him, because who could be? But it really is doubly and trebly hard to have crowds and multitudes turning up now, hoping to take Miss Lucie's affections away from me. There never was nor will be but one man worthy of that sweet girl, and that was my brother Solomon, if he hadn't made a mistake or two in his life.

(Pause)

DARNAY
I see. So... the shoemaker's bench?

MISS PROSS
What about it?

DARNAY
I have been meaning to ask, what is it for?

MISS PROSS
It's the Doctor's. You are aware of his history, yes?

DARNAY
I understand that he spent some time in the Bastille.

MISS PROSS
Almost twenty years, I dare say. That there was his occupation while he was a prisoner.

DARNAY
Does the Doctor ever refer to his shoe-making time?

MISS PROSS
Never.

DARNAY
And yet he keeps the bench and tools at the ready? Do you believe he thinks of it often?

MISS PROSS
Often? I dare say he thinks of it all the time.

DARNAY
Do you imagine--

MISS PROSS
No, I never imagine anything. I have no imagination at all.

DARNAY
Of course. But do you suppose-- You do go so far as to suppose, now and then?

MISS PROSS
Once in a while.

DARNAY
Right. Do you suppose that Doctor Manette has any theory of his own regarding his time in the Bastille?

MISS PROSS
I don't suppose anything about it but what Miss Lucie tells me.

DARNAY
And that is...?

MISS PROSS
She thinks he has. But it's a dreadful remembrance, I should think. Better to leave it alone.

(CARTON enters)

MISS PROSS
Oh, hello there, Mister Carton. Back again?

CARTON
I managed to just miss the rain. How do you do, Miss Pross? *(Noticing DARNAY)* Oh. Darnay. Good to see you again.

DARNAY
And you, Mister Carton. This is a surprise. I wasn't aware that you were acquainted with the Manettes.

CARTON
Yes, well, after your little legal entanglement,

Miss Manette was kind enough to send a note of thanks, and invited me round for tea.

DARNAY
And you accepted. How unexpected.

MISS PROSS
Oh yes. Mister Carton is a regular visitor. Almost as regular as yourself, Mister Darnay.

(LUCIE and DOCTOR MANETTE enter)

MISS PROSS
Ah, here they are!

LUCIE
Hello, Mister Darnay. Mister Carton. So lovely to see you both.

DARNAY
How do you do, Miss Manette, Doctor Manette. I hope it's not an inconvenient time for me to call.

LUCIE
Not at all.

CARTON
You're looking well, Darnay. Freedom agrees with you.

DARNAY
I must say it does. I cannot say the Tower of London does much for one's complexion.

LUCIE
You have quite recovered from your ordeal, then?

DARNAY
I do not know if one ever fully "recovers" from the Tower. But may I say that I have been fortu-

nate in friends to see me through.

LUCIE
You give me too much credit.

DARNAY
Not at all. In truth, I do not know where I would be if not for your generosity and kindness. *(Pause)* And of Doctor Manette's, of course. And Mister Carton.

(CARTON laughs)

DOCTOR MANETTE
Have you seen much of the Tower in your work, Mister Carton?

CARTON
I have. It's not a place I can recommend, history or not.

(CARTON, DOCTOR MANETTE, and MISS PROSS converse. LUCIE speaks to DARNAY. During the following, rain starts falling outside, lightly at first, but harder toward the end)

LUCIE
Was your family relieved to hear of your success, Mister Darnay? *(DARNAY laughs)* I'm sorry. You do not speak of them much.

DARNAY
There is not much to speak of, really. I have an uncle who lives near Paris. We... are not close.

LUCIE
May I ask why not?

DARNAY
A difference in philosophies. My family is an old

one, but our lands are poor. For years the burden has fallen to the people who work the soil. But my family has not been kind to them. It was my mother's hope that one day I might change that, but I fear there is little I can do while my uncle lives.

LUCIE
Your mother's hope? Forgive me, but how can you change anything from England?

DARNAY
Do you wish me to leave?

LUCIE
Not at all! But I have learned, these past five years, that no duty is more sacred than a child's duty to his parents. Your uncle may be intractable, as you say, but do you not owe it to your mother to try?

DARNAY
You have given me much to think about, Miss Manette.

(Another roll of thunder. The guests all stop and take notice)

DOCTOR MANETTE
It's certainly coming down, now. The rain drops are falling large and heavy.

CARTON
It comes slowly.

DOCTOR MANETTE
It comes surely.

(They listen as the rain falls harder)

LUCIE
Is it not impressive, Mister Darnay? I have sometimes sat alone on nights like this, listening to the rain as it echoes through the house. I imagine it to be the sound of all the footsteps that are coming into our lives.

CARTON
There is a great crowd coming, in that case. *(Lightning flashes)* You can see them by the lightning. *(Thunder rolls through)* Here they come, fierce and furious!

(The RESURRECTION MAN enters. The others exit one by one as he speaks)

RESURRECTION MAN
What a night it was! Almost a night to bring the dead out of their graves. Almost. The great bell of Saint Paul's struck one before the night finally cleared. Our friends that night dreamed of a great crowd of people with its rush and roar, bearing down upon them. Let them rest awhile as we move ahead in time and distance. We turn our attention toward Paris, where everyone is dressed for a Fancy Ball they believe will never end. From the Palace to the Court, from the Chambers to the Tribunals of Justice, the Fancy Ball descends even to the Common Executioner, who is required to officiate "frizzled, powdered, in a gold-laced coat, pumps, and white silk stockings." The leprosy of unreality disfigures every human creature in attendance. And through this masquerade, a certain nobleman's carriage drives as though charging an enemy.

(The RESURRECTION MAN exits)

Scene Seven

(We hear the loud clatter of a carriage moving fast on cobblestones as we transition to a Paris street. The carriage comes to a sudden halt as the horses neigh. Crowd noises)

GASPARD
(Off) My child!

(GASPARD enters, carrying a bloody bundle of rags and sobbing. MONSIEUR DEFARGE is with him, followed by MADAME DEFARGE, who watches everything from a distance. The MARQUIS enters separately)

MARQUIS
What is the problem?

MONSIEUR DEFARGE
Pardon, Monsieur the Marquis St. Evremonde! I am afraid your carriage, while navigating this narrow road, struck a small child.

MARQUIS
Why is that man making such an abominable noise? Was it his child?

MONSIEUR DEFARGE
I am afraid it was, Monsieur the Marquis.

(GASPARD *utters a loud cry and steps toward the* MARQUIS, *holding the bloody rags toward him.* MONSIEUR DEFARGE *holds him back)*

MARQUIS
You dog. Take another step toward me and I'll see you crushed under my wheels just like that child.

MONSIEUR DEFARGE
Come Gaspard! Control yourself. Think! It is better for the poor lad to die so, than to live. He died in the span of a moment, without pain. Could he have lived an hour as happily?

(Gradually, GASPARD *gains control of himself)*

MARQUIS
You sound like a philosopher. How do they call you?

MONSIEUR DEFARGE
They call me Defarge.

MARQUIS
What is your trade?

MONSIEUR DEFARGE
I am a vendor of wine.

(The MARQUIS *tosses a coin at* MONSIEUR DEFARGE's *feet)*

MARQUIS
Pick that up, philosopher and vendor of wine,

and spend it as you will. And give this to your companion for his trouble.

(The MARQUIS tosses another coin, then exits. GASPARD starts to charge after him, but MONSIEUR DEFARGE restrains him)

MONSIEUR DEFARGE
Not here, Gaspard. Not now.

GASPARD
Then when? You tell me that!

MADAME DEFARGE
Husband. Let him go.

(MONSIEUR DEFARGE releases GASPARD, who falls to his knees before his child's body. MADAME DEFARGE draws a knife and offers it to GASPARD)

MADAME DEFARGE
Let us take him home, Gaspard.

(After a moment, GASPARD takes the knife. MADAME DEFARGE nods to him. GASPARD exits after the MARQUIS)

MONSIEUR DEFARGE
Why, wife? You send him to certain death. He could have been one of us.

MADAME DEFARGE
He is one of us.

(MADAME DEFARGE picks up the child's body and exits. MONSIEUR DEFARGE lingers a moment. He picks up the coins the MARQUIS tossed, then follows his wife)

Scene Eight

(The scene shifts to the home of the MARQUIS ST. EVREMONDE. The RESURRECTION MAN enters. Over his clothes he has thrown the livery of one of the Marquis' servants. The MARQUIS enters)

MARQUIS
Has my nephew arrived?

RESURRECTION MAN
(French accent) Yes, Monseigneur. Shall I show him in?

MARQUIS
Yes.

RESURRECTION MAN
And shall I set a place for your other guest?

MARQUIS
My what?

RESURRECTION MAN
Your other guest, Monseigneur? Who arrived

with you?

MARQUIS
What the devil are talking about?

RESURRECTION MAN
Forgive me, Monseigneur. Obviously there has been some mistake. Only one of the footmen said he saw another man in the courtyard when you arrived. It is very late, though. He must have seen a shadow.

MARQUIS
Go look out now and tell me if you see anyone.

RESURRECTION MAN
Very good, Monseigneur.

(*The RESURRECTION MAN exits. The MARQUIS draws a dagger from inside his clothing. Reassured of the weapon's presence, he puts it back. The RESURRECTION MAN enters*)

MARQUIS
Well?

RESURRECTION MAN
There is no one, Monseigneur. Nothing but trees and night.

MARQUIS
Fine.

RESURRECTION MAN
Your nephew waits outside, Monseigneur.

MARQUIS
That will be all. (*The RESURRECTION MAN bows and exits*) Charles!

(*DARNAY enters*)

DARNAY
Uncle.

MARQUIS
How long have you been in Paris?

DARNAY
I just arrived.

MARQUIS
From London?

DARNAY
Yes.

MARQUIS
You've been a long time coming.

DARNAY
I was detained, as you well know.

MARQUIS
I'm sure I don't understand. Dare I ask you to explain?

DARNAY
Do you deny that cretin, that John Barsad, was paid by you to perjure himself, in the hopes of keeping me out of France forever?

MARQUIS
Have you any evidence to fortify such an accusation?

DARNAY
I believe that had your influence stretched so far, you would have seen to it that I went to my death, jury or not.

MARQUIS
It is possible. For the honor of the Evremonde

name, I could resolve to inconvenience you to that extent.

DARNAY
Inconvenience! Luckily for me, you are out favor.

MARQUIS
It used not to be so, but France in all such things is changed for the worse. Our ancestors held the right of life and death over the vulgar multitudes. From this room, many such dogs have been taken out to be hanged. One fellow was poniarded on the spot where you now stand. He had the insolence to claim I had taken liberties respecting his sister. Hah! Liberties? I call them my rights as a nobleman of France. Nowadays the assertion of our station might cause us real inconvenience.

DARNAY
We have asserted our station such that I believe the name of Evremonde is more detested than any name in France.

MARQUIS
Let us hope so. Detestation of the high is the involuntary homage of the low. The dark deference of fear and slavery will keep the dogs obedient to the whip. Meanwhile, I will preserve the honor of the family, even if you will not.

DARNAY
The family. Our honorable family, injuring every human creature who comes between us and our pleasure. We are bound to a system that is frightful to me.

MARQUIS
Better to be a rational creature, and accept your destiny.

DARNAY
This place is a crumbling tower of suffering. If it ever becomes mine, it shall be put into hands better qualified to free it from the weight that drags it down. There is a curse on it, and on all this land.

MARQUIS
And so you choose England, then?

DARNAY
I have found refuge there.

MARQUIS
Yes, I have heard that many make that claim. Perhaps you know a compatriot who has also found refuge. A doctor? With his daughter?

DARNAY
What is that to you?

MARQUIS
Why did you come here, nephew?

DARNAY
My mother's last request to me. She wished me to have mercy on the poor people of our land, and to redress the harm we have caused them.

MARQUIS
You certainly took your time about it. Are you certain it has nothing to do with your new friends in England?

DARNAY
You will not speak of them again in my presence.

MARQUIS
Ah. It does, then.

DARNAY
In the few months I have known the Manettes, I have learned more about family and duty than I did in a lifetime as an Evremonde.

(The MARQUIS rings a bell)

MARQUIS
Good night, Charles. I look forward to the pleasure of seeing you again in the morning.

(The RESURRECTION MAN enters, still in the Marquis' livery)

MARQUIS
Light my nephew to his chamber.

DARNAY
No need. I'll not stay here tonight. I have said all I have to say. *(Starts to exit)* Thomas, it is good to see you again.

RESURRECTION MAN
And you, Monsieur Charles.

DARNAY
Goodbye, uncle. *(DARNAY exits, followed by the RESURRECTION MAN)*

(GASPARD enters silently, approaching from behind, armed with a knife. The MARQUIS moves to draw his dagger, but GASPARD gets his knife to the MARQUIS' throat first)

MARQUIS
So there was someone else in the courtyard after all.

GASPARD
Face me. *(The MARQUIS turns and looks at GASPARD)* Do you know me? *(The MARQUIS does not recognize him)* You killed my son. You ran him down in the road, like a dog. This very day, you did so.

MARQUIS
You know you will never leave this place alive.

GASPARD
What's that to me?

MARQUIS
Perhaps we can come to some sort of arrangement.

GASPARD
You think I want money?

MARQUIS
Everything has a price.

(GASPARD stabs the MARQUIS)

GASPARD
For my son.

(The MARQUIS dies. GASPARD takes out a piece of paper and drops it next to the MARQUIS' body. GASPARD exits. The RESURRECTION MAN enters, without the livery. He is not surprised to find the body. He picks up the paper)

RESURRECTION MAN
(Cockney accent) "Drive him fast to his tomb. From Jacques." O Justice! The first blow is struck against Tyranny!

(The scene shifts to the Defarges' wine shop)

RESURRECTION MAN
Well, that's one way to look at it. You might look at it another when you learn that Monsieur the Marquis was right. Poor Gaspard was caught before he left the estate. Bound hand and foot, his mouth gagged with a tight string, making him look almost as if he laughed, he was led to the town square. A gallows was built above the fountain where the women and children drew water. There Gaspard was hanged, and left dangling for the world to see, poisoning the water below.

(MONSIEUR DEFARGE and JACQUES #1 enter, followed by MADAME DEFARGE, knitting)

JACQUES #1
Well, Jacques? We have seen the fate of our comrade. What say the others?

MONSIEUR DEFARGE
It is the same everywhere, Jacques. Our friend Gaspard was just another stick of kindling in the bonfire. But the fire rises, my friends. And when the time is right, the tyrants will burn.

JACQUES #1
Shall I tell the others we are ready to join with them?

MONSIEUR DEFARGE
What do you think?

JACQUES #1
I cannot say.

MONSIEUR DEFARGE
(to the RESURRECTION MAN) What say you, Jacques?

RESURRECTION MAN
(French accent) What says Madame?

(All three turn to MADAME DEFARGE, who continues to knit)

MADAME DEFARGE
I say, that although it is a long time on the road, it is coming. I say it never retreats, never stops, always advancing. Look around and consider the lives of all the world that we know. Consider the faces. Consider the rage and discontent to which the Jacquerie addresses itself with more and more certainty every hour. And still you must look to me for an answer? Nothing we do is done in vain. I believe, with all my soul, that we shall triumph.

MONSIEUR DEFARGE
Then tell them, Jacques. When the time comes, the Quarter Saint Antoine shall answer the call.

JACQUES #1
They shall look to you, afterward. France will need wise men like you.

MONSIEUR DEFARGE
All I am, for the citizens of France.

(JACQUES #1 embraces MONSIEUR DEFARGE and exits)

RESURRECTION MAN
(referring to Madame Defarge's knitting) You work hard, madame.

MADAME DEFARGE
I have a good deal to do.

RESURRECTION MAN
What do you make, madame?

MADAME DEFARGE
Many things.

RESURRECTION MAN
For instance?

MADAME DEFARGE
For instance, shrouds.

RESURRECTION MAN
Au revoir, madame. *(exits)*

MADAME DEFARGE
Wise men like you.

MONSIEUR DEFARGE
Wife, you know I defer to you in all things.

MADAME DEFARGE
What of Evremonde?

MONSIEUR DEFARGE
The Marquis is dead.

MADAME DEFARGE
The man who was the Marquis is dead. The man who is now the Marquis still lives.

MONSIEUR DEFARGE
Charles Darnay is on his way back to England. He has abandoned his name and title. He has given over the managing of his estate to his servant Gabelle, a good man--

MADAME DEFARGE
Charles Darnay is an Evremonde.

MONSIEUR DEFARGE
He is not his uncle. Or his father.

MADAME DEFARGE
Punish the children for the sins of the fathers to the third and fourth generation.

MONSIEUR DEFARGE
The desires of one citizen cannot come before the needs of France.

MADAME DEFARGE
Tell me, then, that France will not be served by the extermination of that family.

MONSIEUR DEFARGE
But why that family? Who are these men to you?

MADAME DEFARGE
By God, husband, I will have my way in this.

MONSIEUR DEFARGE
Very well, wife. When the day comes, God help the heir of Evremonde.

(They exit)

Scene Nine

(CARTON enters. He finds a quiet corner, and drinks from a flask. The RESURRECTION MAN enters)

RESURRECTION MAN
Mister Carton, sir. What brings you round to the Manettes' at this time of night?

CARTON
I have been ruminating. I have found a wonderful fact to reflect upon.

RESURRECTION MAN
And what is that, sir?

CARTON
That every human creature is constituted to be a profound mystery to every other. A solemn consideration, when I travel this great city by night, that every one of those darkly clustered houses encloses its own secret; that every room in every one of them encloses its own secret; that

each of those hundreds of thousands of beating hearts is, in some way or another, a secret to the heart nearest it. What do you think?

RESURRECTION MAN
I can find no fault in it, to be sure.

CARTON
The houses are like mausoleums. Think of it. In any cemetery in this city, is there a sleeper more inscrutable to me than any waking inhabitant is? Or me to them?

(CARTON takes one last drink from his flask, puts it away, and starts to exit)

RESURRECTION MAN
Are you sure that's a good idea, Mister Carton?

(CARTON pauses, as if unsure who spoke to him. He chooses to ignore the voice, and exits. The RESURRECTION MAN watches him go, then follows)

Scene Ten

(The scene shifts to the London home of LUCIE and DOCTOR MANETTE. CARTON enters and finds LUCIE there)

LUCIE
Mister Carton?

CARTON
Pray forgive me, Miss Manette. I know it is very late.

LUCIE
Is there something you want?

CARTON
I don't know quite how to say what it is that I want to say to you.

LUCIE
Whatever you have to say, if it will do you any good, then I will be quite happy to hear it.

CARTON
If it had been possible that you could have returned

the love of the man you see before yourself - poor, drunken creature of misuse as you know him to be - he would be conscious, in spite of his happiness, that he would bring you to misery. I know very well that you can have no tenderness for me. I ask for none. I am even thankful that it cannot be.

LUCIE
Will nothing of this happiness remain?

CARTON
No. All through it I knew myself to be quite undeserving. What is to be expected of, or by, such profligates?

LUCIE
Since it is my misfortune to have made you more unhappy than you were before you knew me--

CARTON
Don't say that. You would have reclaimed me, if you could. You will not be the cause of my becoming worse.

LUCIE
But since your current state is, as you describe, attributable to me, then have I no power for good with you?

CARTON
All you can ever do for me is done. Since I knew you I have been troubled by a remorse that I thought would never reproach me again. I have heard whispers from old voices impelling me upward, that I thought were silent forever. I have had unformed ideas of beginning anew, striving afresh, fighting out the long-abandoned fight. All a dream, ending in nothing, leaving the sleeper

where he lay down. But I wish you to know that you inspired it.

LUCIE
Mister Carton...

CARTON
I am not worth such feeling. An hour or two hence, and the low habits that I scorn, but yield to, will render me less worth such tears than any wretch who creeps along the streets. But there is one thing you can do for me.

LUCIE
Anything, if I can.

CARTON
Try to hold me in your mind, at some quiet time, as ardent and sincere in this one thing: For you, and for any dear to you, I would do anything. I would embrace any sacrifice. Think of this, now and then.

LUCIE
I will.

CARTON
I am distressing you. I will come to an end. When I remember this day, will you let me believe that this last confidence of my life lies with you alone, and will be shared by no one?

LUCIE
The secret is yours, not mine. I promise to respect it.

CARTON
Thank you. Be under no apprehension of my ever resuming this conversation again, even in passing.

I will never refer to it again.

LUCIE
I know you would say this to no one else. Can I in no way repay your confidence?

(CARTON almost attempts to kiss LUCIE; she almost lets him. He stops himself and kisses her hand instead)

CARTON
Farewell, Miss Manette.

(CARTON exits, leaving LUCIE alone on stage)

Scene Eleven

(The next day, at the Manettes' home. CHARLES enters from outside. DOCTOR MANETTE enters and greets him)

DOCTOR MANETTE
Charles Darnay, back from France so soon? I rejoice to see you. Miss Manette is paying a visit to a neighbor, but will soon be home. She will be delighted you have returned.

DARNAY
Actually, Doctor Manette, I took the opportunity of her being from home, that I might speak to you.

DOCTOR MANETTE
Oh dear. Your first day home from France and I am the first person you call upon? I think I should like to sit down for this. *(He does so)* Very well. Please proceed.

DARNAY
Doctor Manette, I am sure you anticipate what

I am about to say, though you cannot know how earnestly I say it. Dear sir, I love your daughter fondly, dearly, devotedly. If ever there was love in the world, I love her.

DOCTOR MANETTE
I believe you. Have you spoken to Lucie?

DARNAY
No.

DOCTOR MANETTE
Nor written?

DARNAY
I have not.

DOCTOR MANETTE
Have you any reason to believe that Lucie loves you?

DARNAY
None, as yet.

DOCTOR MANETTE
What do you seek from me, then?

DARNAY
I understand well that even if Miss Manette held me in her heart at this very moment, I could not hope to hold that place long against her love for her father. I understand equally well that a word from her father, in any suitor's favor, would outweigh herself in all the world.

DOCTOR MANETTE
And you want me to give that word?

DARNAY
On the contrary, Doctor Manette. I would not ask that word of you to save my life.

DOCTOR MANETTE
Well then. Charles Darnay, mysteries arise out of close love. They are subtle and delicate, and difficult to penetrate. In this one respect, my daughter Lucie is such a mystery to me. I can make no guess at the state of her heart.

DARNAY
I see. May I ask you one favor?

DOCTOR MANETTE
That depends on what it is.

DARNAY
Just this. If Miss Manette should, on her own part, bring to you such a confidence as the one I have just laid before you, you will bear testimony to what I have said, and your belief in it. I hope you think well enough of me that you will not influence her against me.

DOCTOR MANETTE
I promise. If Lucie should ever tell me that you are essential to her perfect happiness... even if there were any... apprehensions...

DARNAY
Apprehensions? Doctor Manette, if you have any objections--

DOCTOR MANETTE
No. No objections. It is just that... I have seen your face before, young man.

DARNAY
Yes. We met on the ferry from Calais, when you first came here from France.

(Pause)

DOCTOR MANETTE
Yes. Calais.

DARNAY
Doctor Manette, your confidence in me ought to be returned with full disclosure on my part. My present name, Darnay, was my mother's. I wish to tell you my own name, and why I am in England.

DOCTOR MANETTE
Stop.

DARNAY
Sir, I wish there to be no secrets between us.

DOCTOR MANETTE
Stop!

(DOCTOR MANETTE presses both hands against his ears. DARNAY is silent)

DOCTOR MANETTE
Tell me when I ask you. Not now. If your suit should prosper, if Lucie should love you, tell me then. Do you promise?

DARNAY
Willingly.

DOCTOR MANETTE
Good. Now, you must excuse me. I hear her coming, and I would prefer it if she did not find us conspiring. I will leave you alone so you may speak with her.

DARNAY
Thank you, Doctor Manette.

(DOCTOR MANETTE exits, leaving DARNAY alone. He braces himself as he hears LUCIE and

MISS PROSS enter)

LUCIE
Mister Darnay? When did you return from France?

DARNAY
This very day, Miss Manette. I have not even returned to my own rooms, yet.

LUCIE
You came straight here?

DARNAY
I did. I have something I wish to discuss with you.

(Pause)

LUCIE
Miss Pross, would you--

MISS PROSS
Why don't I go check on the Doctor?

LUCIE
Yes, thank you. *(MISS PROSS exits)* What can I do for you, Mister Darnay?

DARNAY
You can call me Charles. And if I may be so bold, I would like your permission to call you Lucie.

LUCIE
I see.

DARNAY
Miss Manette... I love you. What other men may mean when they use that expression, I cannot tell. What I mean, is that you could draw me to fire, draw me to the gallows, draw me to any exposure and disgrace, if only you would return a favorable answer to my offer.

LUCIE
What offer is that?

DARNAY
I mean myself. In marriage.

LUCIE
I don't know what to say.

DARNAY
Whatever considerations I may have thought of against this offer, I have conquered them, and I make it with all my heart. I may only be a tutor, but you would want for nothing, and if you saw me at my work you would see I am able to do it well, and am respected in it. You might even come to take a sort of pride in me. I would try hard that you should. I only add that if it is any claim on you to be earnest, then I am in earnest, most thorough and most dreadful.

LUCIE
I know it. And I confess, I had hoped for this day. And now that it is here... Mister Darnay, you remember when I told you there was no duty more sacred than a child's duty to his parents?

DARNAY
I do.

LUCIE
You understand, then, the duty I feel toward my father.

DARNAY
I have observed it often.

LUCIE
All my life, there was this ache inside me. I never

understood it. I could not speak to my mother about it, or Miss Pross. But then the letter came from across the sea, telling me my father lived, that he needed me... and the ache was gone. I have spent the past five years bringing my father back to life, and knowing him has allowed me to know myself. Just the thought that anything might come between us now...

DARNAY
If I ever thought that I might cause any sort of separation between you and your father, I never would have considered even coming here today. I am, like the Doctor, a voluntary exile from France. Like him, I strive to live away from it by my own exertions, and trusting in a happier future. I look only to share your fortunes, share your life and home, and to be faithful to you to the death. I would never divide you from your privilege as his daughter, companion, and friend. I would strive rather to bind you closer to him, if such a thing was possible.

LUCIE
Mister Darnay, I will treasure the sweet words of love you have spoken to me, but it was these last words I truly longed to hear.

DARNAY
I... I do not know that I could say any more if I tried.

LUCIE
You have said so much. I feel compelled to deliver my response with equal verbosity.

DARNAY
I shall happily listen to your answer for as long as

you require, Miss Manette.

LUCIE
I think... I think I should quite like it if you would call me Lucie. *(They exit)*

(Lights shift to the shoemaker's bench, that evening. DOCTOR MANETTE enters and sits down. He looks at his tools, examines the materials, but does not start to work. MISS PROSS enters and sees him. DOCTOR MANETTE puts down the materials as if caught doing something he shouldn't. He exits. MISS PROSS is left looking at the bench)

Scene Twelve

(The scene shifts to a London street. The RESURRECTION MAN enters, carrying a shovel and a crowbar. In the background, PALL BEARERS carry on a plain pine coffin, deposit it unceremoniously, and exit. A PRIEST mimes a brief, half-hearted prayer and then exits)

RESURRECTION MAN
You will all remember Mister John Barsad, the fellow who made a hash of testifying against our Mister Darnay earlier? Well, apparently, he went and died. He was mourned by few, and not for very long. The man had a reputation, as it were.
(Indicating the tools) What, these? It's work for an honest tradesman like myself. Work, for the Resurrection Man. *(He approaches the coffin and begins to work at the lid with the crowbar)* Now, what is a Resurrection Man? As I say, he's a tradesman. He trades in a branch of scientific goods. When you go to your doctor and tell 'em you've got a pain right here in the whoozits, and

he answers back, "Why, that's your pancreas!", you can thank the Resurrection Man for providing him with the tools to improve his knowledge of anatomy. Now I know you're asking yourself, but how can I become a Resurrection Man? Well, it all comes down to two things: A keen eye for quality specimens... and the ability to keep your mouth shut. *(The lid comes off. The coffin is empty)* Well now, that is unusual. Where O where, one wonders, is Mister John Barsad?

(BARSAD enters as the scene shifts to Paris. The RESURRECTION MAN stows his tools in the coffin)

BARSAD
You are called Jacques?

RESURRECTION MAN
(French accent) We are all called Jacques, Monsieur. It is our nom de guerre.

BARSAD
And this wine shop owner, Ernest Defarge, he is your leader?

RESURRECTION MAN
Not a leader, as such. He holds tight to our reins, lest the Jacquerie lose control.

BARSAD
And is he called "Jacques" as well?

RESURRECTION MAN
By us, yes. You may try, but he will not be trapped so easily.

BARSAD
I have no intention of trapping him.

RESURRECTION MAN
What, may I ask, do you intend to do?

BARSAD
He holds the reins of the Jacquerie, you say? My instructions are to make him loosen his grip.

RESURRECTION MAN
Why would the aristocracy want that?

BARSAD
"Why" has never been my concern. But I imagine they hope you will do something foolish, and give them the excuse to round up and hang the lot of you. Don't worry, though. *(BARSAD holds out a coin purse)* I'll see to it you don't end up on their list. *(The RESURRECTION MAN reaches for the purse; BARSAD draws it back)* Where is this wine shop?

RESURRECTION MAN
The Quarter Saint Antoine. *(BARSAD hands over the coin purse, and exits. The RESURRECTION MAN resumes his Cockney accent)* No need to worry. It's too late for him to do any real damage. Even as he makes his way to the Quarter Saint Antoine, a mob gathers outside the Chaussée-d'Antin. An hour from now, everything will change. Let us observe these last few moments before the world turns upside down. *(He exits)*

Scene Thirteen

(The scene shifts to the Defarges' wine shop. MONSIEUR and MADAME DEFARGE sit with the SEAMSTRESS, who is visibly upset. MADAME DEFARGE consoles her)

SEAMSTRESS
I'm sorry. I just didn't know where else to turn.

MADAME DEFARGE
You were right to come to us.

SEAMSTRESS
He's... he's dead now. Isn't he?

MADAME DEFARGE
Your husband? Yes. Almost certainly.

MONSIEUR DEFARGE
The Marquis never intended to let him go. You must have realized that.

SEAMSTRESS
I know that now. I just hoped... I didn't believe

he could be so ruthless.

MADAME DEFARGE
That was foolish. He was an aristocrat, and worse, he was an Evremonde. The world will be a better place when that race is wiped from the face of the earth.

SEAMSTRESS
No one will look me in the face, but I feel their eyes on my back as I pass. I hear the whispers. I cannot find work. So many have closed their doors to me. Everyone but you.

(MADAME DEFARGE gives a smile that does not reach her eyes)

MONSIEUR DEFARGE
Do you have any family you can go to?

SEAMSTRESS
I have a cousin in Orleans. We were very close as children, but I have not seen her in some time.

MONSIEUR DEFARGE
Perhaps now would be a good time to write to her.

SEAMSTRESS
I should go. Thank you, Madame Defarge. Monsieur.

MONSIEUR DEFARGE
It is late. I shall walk you home. Wait for me one moment. *(The SEAMSTRESS exits)* Well?

MADAME DEFARGE
You heard her story.

MONSIEUR DEFARGE
You don't believe her?

MADAME DEFARGE
I believe every word of it. She is not clever enough to lie.

MONSIEUR DEFARGE
It is an understandable mistake, then.

MADAME DEFARGE
She let Evremonde take her to his bed.

MONSIEUR DEFARGE
She believed she could free her husband. Do not add her name to the list for that.

(In response, MADAME DEFARGE takes up her knitting and begins to work)

MONSIEUR DEFARGE
Very well. I shall return shortly.

(MONSIEUR DEFARGE exits. For a moment there is nothing but the clicking of Madame Defarge's knitting. BARSAD enters. MADAME DEFARGE pauses just long enough to give the newcomer a once-over, then resumes knitting)

BARSAD
Good day, madame.

MADAME DEFARGE
Good day, monsieur.

BARSAD
Might I trouble you for a glass of old cognac, madame?

(MADAME DEFARGE puts down her knitting, gets a glass, pours the drink, and sets it down on the bar in front of BARSAD. He takes a drink)

BARSAD
Marvelous cognac, madame!

MADAME DEFARGE
The cognac is flattered.

BARSAD
You knit with great skill, madame. A pretty pattern, too! May one ask what it is for?

MADAME DEFARGE
It is a pastime.

BARSAD
Not for use?

MADAME DEFARGE
I will use it one day.

BARSAD
Business seems bad.

MADAME DEFARGE
Business is bad. The people are poor.

BARSAD
Ah, the unfortunate people! So oppressed, as you say.

MADAME DEFARGE
As I say?

BARSAD
Pardon me. Certainly it was I who said so, but that is what everyone is thinking.

MADAME DEFARGE
I and my husband have enough to do to keep this wine shop open, without thinking. All we think, here, is how to live.

(Pause as BARSAD thinks of another tack)

BARSAD
A bad business, Gaspard's execution, no? Poor Gaspard!

MADAME DEFARGE
If people use knives for such purposes, they have to pay for it. He knew the price of his luxury beforehand, and he has paid it.

BARSAD
I believe there is some real anger in this neighborhood regarding this poor fellow.

MADAME DEFARGE
Is there?

(MONSIEUR DEFARGE enters)

BARSAD
Ah, good day, Jacques!

(MONSIEUR DEFARGE appears perplexed, and continues about his business)

BARSAD
I say, good day, Jacques!

MONSIEUR DEFARGE
You mistake, sir. My name is Ernest Defarge.

BARSAD
Pardon me. I must have been misinformed. I was saying to madame when you entered that they tell me there is much anger and sympathy for poor Gaspard here in the Quarter Saint Antoine.

MONSIEUR DEFARGE
You seem to know this quarter well. Better than I do.

BARSAD
Not at all, but I hope to know it better. The pleasure of conversing with you reminds me that I have the honor of cherishing some interesting associations with your name, Monsieur Defarge.

MONSIEUR DEFARGE
Indeed.

BARSAD
Yes indeed. When Doctor Alexandre Manette was released, you, being his old servant, were given charge of him.

MONSIEUR DEFARGE
Such is the fact, certainly.

BARSAD
It was to you that his daughter came, and it was from you that his daughter took him to England. Very interesting remembrances!

MONSIEUR DEFARGE
Oh yes?

BARSAD
Yes. You don't hear much from them now?

MONSIEUR DEFARGE
No.

BARSAD
Then perhaps you will be surprised to learn that the daughter is going to be married?

MADAME DEFARGE
Going? She was pretty enough to be married long ago. You English are cold, it seems to me.

BARSAD
Well. Yes, I say Miss Manette is going to be married. But not to an Englishman. Rather, she is to marry one who, like herself, is French by birth. And speaking of poor, poor Gaspard, it is a curious thing that she is going to marry the nephew of Monsieur the Marquis, the one for whom Gaspard was so... elevated. In other words, she will marry the present Marquis. But he lives unknown in England. He is no Marquis there. He is simply Mister Charles Darnay. He takes his name from his mother's family, I hear. *(BARSAD finishes his drink and drops a coin on the counter)* Thanks for that. *(He exits)*

MADAME DEFARGE
That was him?

MONSIEUR DEFARGE
He's the one that Jacques in the police warned us about, John Barsad. The aristocracy have sunk so low as to hire an Englishman as their agent provocateur. You must add him to the list.

MADAME DEFARGE
Not yet. Men such as him serve their purposes.

MONSIEUR DEFARGE
What purpose could possibly be served by a worm like that? *(MADAME DEFARGE gives him a look)* Very well. Can what he said of Mademoiselle Manette be true?

MADAME DEFARGE
It may be.

MONSIEUR DEFARGE
If it be so, I hope for her sake that Destiny will

keep her husband out of France.

MADAME DEFARGE
Her husband's destiny will lead him to the end that ends him.

(JACQUES #1 enters, urgent)

JACQUES #1
Have you heard? Rioting has broken out in the Chausséed'Antin. Two of the King's cavalry are dead.

MONSIEUR DEFARGE
What? The whole city will be in chaos by morning! We are not ready!

JACQUES #1
We have thirty thousand muskets from the Hôtel des Invalides. All we need are powder and shot.

(Pause as MONSIEUR DEFARGE realizes the ramifications)

MONSIEUR DEFARGE
There is only one place we can find what we need.

MADAME DEFARGE
Husband, it is time.

MONSIEUR DEFARGE
Yes. *(To JACQUES #1)* Gather everyone. You know what to do.

JACQUES #1
Have we lit the flame, Jacques?

MONSIEUR DEFARGE
Yes, Jacques. The fire rises.

Scene Fourteen

(The RESURRECTION MAN enters)

RESURRECTION MAN
It has been remarked that the corner on which the Doctor and Lucie lived was a wonderful spot for echoes. One could sit in the still house and listen to the echoing footsteps of time. There was something coming, in those echoes. Something far off and scarcely audible yet it stirred the heart. Fluttering hopes and doubts, like waves upon a sea.

(LUCIE and DARNAY enter hand in hand. They approach DOCTOR MANETTE)

RESURRECTION MAN
We hear the echo as Charles Darnay fulfills his promise, and speaks a name no one wished to hear:

RESURRECTION MAN & DARNAY
Evremonde.

(DOCTOR MANETTE looks to his shoemaker's bench. He makes a decision, turns back, and takes DARNAY's hand. They exit)

RESURRECTION MAN
While a new sun dawns over one city, dark clouds gather over the other. The skies threaten, the waves grow higher, and in the Quarter Saint Antoine the waters boil and rage in a whirlpool that circles around the Defarge's wine shop, and every human drop on the maelstrom is sucked toward the vortex where Defarge himself labors in the thickest of the uproar.

(MONSIEUR DEFARGE and MADAME DEFARGE enter, followed by JACQUES #1 and several other REVOLUTIONARIES, all wearing red caps and armed with whatever type of weapon they can find)

MONSIEUR DEFARGE
Keep near to me, Jacques! Put yourself at the head of as many of these patriots as you can! Where will you be, wife?

MADAME DEFARGE
You shall see me at the head of the women, by and by.

MONSIEUR DEFARGE
Come then! Patriots and friends, we are ready! To the Bastille!

ALL
To the Bastille!

(The REVOLUTIONARIES begins to sing "La Carmagnole," quietly at first, underneath the Resurrection Man's dialogue, then building to a crescendo)

RESURRECTION MAN

The living sea rises, wave on wave, depth on depth, and overflows the city. Alarm bells ring, drums beat, the sea rages and thunders on its new beach, and the footsteps of Saint Antoine echo through the Paris streets in mid-July, One Thousand Seven Hundred and Eighty-Nine. For I am the resurrection and the life, saith the Lord. He that believeth in me, though he were dead, yet shall he live, and whosoever liveth and believeth in me, shall never die.

REVOLUTIONARIES

Madame Veto avait promis,
Madame Veto avait promis.
de faire égorger tout Paris,
de faire égorger tout Paris.
Mais son coup a manqué
grâce à nos canonniers.
Dansons la Carmagnole
Vive le son,
Vive le son.
Dansons la Carmagnole
Vive le son du canon.

(MADAME DEFARGE spots the SEAMSTRESS in the crowd and points to her)

MADAME DEFARGE

Conspirateur!

(The crowd picks up the cry and attacks the SEAMSTRESS, grabbing her roughly and dragging her off. They continue singing)

REVOLUTIONARIES

Monsieur Veto avait promis,
Monsieur Veto avait promis.

D'être fidèle à son pays,
D'être fidèle à son pays.
Mais il y a manqué,
Ne faisons plus quartier.
Dansons la Carmagnole
Vive le son,
Vive le son.
Dansons la Carmagnole
Vive le son du canon.

(The RESURRECTION MAN joins in the song at the end. There is a explosion of gun and cannon fire. When the smoke clears, the RESURRECTION MAN stands alone in a sea of corpses)

RESURRECTION MAN
And so it begins.

END OF ACT ONE

ACT II

Scene Fifteen

(Lights up on the Manettes' home. LUCIE and DARNAY celebrate their engagement with DOCTOR MANETTE, MISS PROSS, and CARTON, who takes DARNAY aside)

CARTON
To your future wife, and to the honor of your noble name. You are a better man than I, sir. *(He drinks)* Mister Darnay, I wish we might be friends.

DARNAY
We are already friends, I hope.

CARTON
You are good enough to say so, as a fashion of speech, but I don't mean any fashion of speech. Indeed, when I say I wish we might be friends, I scarcely mean quite that, either.

DARNAY
My dear fellow... What do you mean?

CARTON
Upon my life, I find that easier to comprehend in my own mind than to convey to yours. But let me try. You remember a certain famous occasion when I was more drunk than... than usual?

DARNAY
I remember a certain famous occasion when you forced me to confess that you had been drinking.

CARTON
The curse of those occasions is heavy upon me, for I always remember them. I hope it may be taken into account one day. On the drunken occasion in question - one of a large number, as you know - I was insufferable about liking you, and not liking you. I wish you would forget it.

DARNAY
I forgot it long ago.

CARTON
Fashion of speech again! But I have by no means forgotten it, and a light answer from you does not help me to forget it.

DARNAY
If it was a light answer, I beg your forgiveness for it. I declare to you, on the faith of a gentleman, that I have long dismissed it from my mind. Good Heaven, what was there to dismiss? You rendered me a great service that day!

CARTON
A great service. Mere professional claptrap. I don't know that I cared what became of you when I rendered it.

DARNAY
Now it is you who gives a light answer.

CARTON
You are distracting me from the point. I was speaking about our being friends. You know me as a man incapable of all the higher and better flights of men; who has never done any good, and never will.

DARNAY
You have done good, whether you meant to or no. And I'm certain I don't know that you "never will" again.

CARTON
What if I am certain?

DARNAY
You are not. You cannot be. You say you did not care what became of me when you defended me in court? Well let me tell you something: I don't believe it. Nor do I believe this facade you have created for yourself, this picture of a dissolute dog which you employ for reasons I'm sure I don't understand, but it saves you the trouble of honest communion with your fellow man. One day, Mister Carton, you will find something to bring out the very best in you. You will show us all what a great man you can be. More important, you will show yourself.

(*DARNAY offers his hand to CARTON, who takes it. They shake. DARNAY exits. CARTON goes to take another drink, and finds his flask empty. CARTON exits*)

Scene Sixteen

(The sounds of rioting and violence. Lights up on a cell in the Bastille. The RESURRECTION MAN enters, wearing the red cap of a revolutionary)

RESURRECTION MAN
We leave now England's green and pleasant land, and turn our story once again to France. Far and wide lay a ruined country, yielding nothing but desolation. Every green leaf, every blade of grass and grain, was shriveled and poor as the miserable people. Everything was bowed down, dejected, oppressed, and broken. Habitations, fences, animals, men, women, children, and the soil that bore them, all worn out. And who is to blame? The ruling class, of course; those that bear such exalted and ancient names as Evremonde. But the current Marquis, our hero Charles Darnay, had returned to England. Where, then, shall the People turn their rage, if the Monseigneur be not at home to answer it?

(*The sound of a door being smashed open. REVOLUTIONARIES burst in, Including JACQUES #1. MADAME DEFARGE stands in the doorway*)

MADAME DEFARGE
This is it. One hundred and five, North Tower. Look everywhere. Tear up the stones if you have to.

JACQUES #1
What are we looking for?

MADAME DEFARGE
I will know it when I see it.

(*The REVOLUTIONARIES tear through the cell, searching for something. One of the Revolutionaries pulls up a stone in the floor. From beneath it he pulls up several bits of aged paper. JACQUES #1 takes it from him and brings it to MADAME DEFARGE*)

JACQUES #1
Madame.

(*MADAME DEFARGE takes the papers and reads them. The others wait expectantly. MONSIEUR DEFARGE enters. MADAME DEFARGE does not acknowledge him, but exits with the letter*)

MONSIEUR DEFARGE
(*to the REVOLUTIONARIES*) Come. There is more work to be done.

(*MONSIEUR DEFARGE & the REVOLUTIONARIES exit. The RESURRECTION MAN removes his cap and puts on the Marquis' livery*)

RESURRECTION MAN
In England, the well-to-do commiserate with their counterparts in France, and thank the stars their own revolution remained comfortably across the Atlantic. An embarrassment, perhaps. But at least no one lost their head over it. In France, for many, keeping one's head was a difficult game to play. You will remember poor Thomas Gabelle, servant to the late Marquis. We find him now in dire straits.

(The scene shifts to reveal DARNAY and DOCTOR MANETTE. DARNAY reads the letter as the RESURRECTION MAN narrates it)

RESURRECTION MAN
"Monsieur the Marquis: I have been seized, with great violence and indignity, and brought on foot to Paris. The crime for which I am imprisoned, and for which I may lose my life, is the treason of acting on your behalf. I have tried in vain to explain that, according to your instructions, I acted for the people, and not against them. The only response from them is, Where is the Marquis? And so I send my desolate cry across the sea, hoping it may reach your ears. My only fault is that I have been true to you. I pray, Monsieur the Marquis, that you will be true to me. From this prison of horrors, where every hour brings me nearer to destruction, I send you the assurance of my dolorous and unhappy service. Yours afflicted, Gabelle." *(exits)*

DOCTOR MANETTE
Who is Gabelle?

DARNAY
My steward. After my uncle's death, I employed him to oversee the Evremonde estate.

DOCTOR MANETTE
It could be a snare.

DARNAY
Perhaps. But I do not doubt that Gabelle wrote the note. And given his position, he has almost certainly been arrested. And that is my doing.

DOCTOR MANETTE
Yours? How?

DARNAY
I believe you know that my family in France has a reputation. My uncle, my father, his father... I chose to renounce my station rather than uphold the crumbling fabric of that world. But though my renunciation was complete in my own mind, I should have formally worked out the transition. I meant to do so, but in the joy I found in my new life in London I kept finding reasons to delay, and delay... and now another man may pay for my idleness with his life.

DOCTOR MANETTE
Charles, you cannot go to Paris. Have you not heard the reports coming from there? No one is safe; certainly no one with ties to the aristocracy. There are rumors of twenty executions a day.

DARNAY
I have no choice.

DOCTOR MANETTE
You are about to be married. Lucie will not understand.

DARNAY
She will. I know it.

DOCTOR MANETTE
You would throw your life away for this man?

DARNAY
It will not come to that.

DOCTOR MANETTE
The Loadstone Rock is drawing you, and you will sail on until you strike it.

DARNAY
I see little danger in that. If I can but make my intentions understood, I believe what I have done will be gratefully received in France.

DOCTOR MANETTE
You are resolved, then?

DARNAY
I am.

DOCTOR MANETTE
I believe I understand, now, why my daughter chose you. Come, my son. I will stand by you when you break the news.

(They exit)

Scene Seventeen

(The Resurrection Man enters as the scene shifts to Lucie's dressing room. Lucie is in her wedding gown. Miss Pross frets over her, trying to keep from sobbing)

RESURRECTION MAN
The morning of the marriage day shone brightly. For Miss Pross, the event would have been, through a gradual process of reconcilement to the inevitable, one of absolute bliss, but for the lingering consideration that her brother Solomon should have been the bridegroom.

LUCIE
Dear Miss Pross, please don't cry. If you start then I won't be able to help myself, and there will be no end to it.

MISS PROSS
It's nothing, Miss Lucie. Merely a... a gift that was delivered last night. A present of plate, lovely enough to bring tears to one's eyes. Indeed, there's

not fork or spoon in the collection that I didn't cry over.

(MISS PROSS bursts into tears)

LUCIE
Isn't there anything that can be done?

(MISS PROSS pulls it together)

MISS PROSS
I shall bring them in and unpack them, then see that the silver is polished and ready for your return. Hurry now, Miss Lucie. The carriage will be here any minute.

(MISS PROSS rushes out, almost knocking into DOCTOR MANETTE as he enters)

RESURRECTION MAN
It is an occasion that makes a man speculate on all he has lost.

DOCTOR MANETTE
May I enter?

LUCIE
Of course, Father!

(DOCTOR MANETTE enters, and stops short when he sees his daughter)

LUCIE
You are happy, Father?

DOCTOR MANETTE
Quite, my child. But more important, are you happy? I cannot say I like it, Charles planning to leave so soon after. Why not postpone the wedding until he returns from France?

LUCIE
He suggested that as well. And I told him what I shall now tell you. We shall do no such thing.

DOCTOR MANETTE
But are you not afraid? The news from Paris--

LUCIE
All the more reason, Father. Charles is a good man. That is why I would have him for my husband. That is why he must go to France now. And that is why I am not afraid. I just hope... Can you tell me that you are sure, quite sure, that my marriage to Charles will never come between us? I know it well, but do you know it?

DOCTOR MANETTE
Quite sure! More than that, I feel my future to be brighter now than it ever could have been before.

LUCIE
Oh, I hope so, Father.

DOCTOR MANETTE
Believe it, Lucie. I have long felt that your life should not be wasted for my sake.

LUCIE
If I had never seen Charles, I should have been quite happy, just the two of us.

DOCTOR MANETTE
But you did see Charles. And if it had not been him, it would have been another. And if no other, that would mean the darkest part of my life had cast its shadow on you, and I could not bear that. *(LUCIE takes DOCTOR MANETTE's hand)* You were not yet born when I was taken away. For eighteen years I speculated upon the child I

never knew. I often wondered whether it was a daughter. Sometimes I pictured her as perfectly ignorant and unconscious of me, as though I had altogether perished from the remembrance of the living. But then there were other times, when I imagined her coming to me in my cell, and leading me out into freedom. I imagined her showing me her home. My picture was in her room, and I was in her prayers.

LUCIE
I was that child, father. I was not half so good, but in my love that was I.

DOCTOR MANETTE
My dear, you are neither of those. Naught that I imagined could compare to the joy you bring me, every day of my life.

(MISS PROSS enters)

MISS PROSS
It's time, miss!

Scene Eighteen

(The RESURRECTION MAN enters)

RESURRECTION MAN
It was a lovely ceremony, as you can imagine. Miss Pross wept, and then wept some more as the carriage departed, conveying Charles Darnay south.

(DARNAY enters. As he travels, he gradually collects an entourage of red-capped REVOLUTIONARIES who continually examine his papers and search his clothes and belongings)

RESURRECTION MAN
The journey from London to Paris was a slow one in the best of times, with more than enough of bad roads and bad horses, but the changed times were fraught with other obstacles than these. Every town and village had its band of citizen patriots stopping and questioning all comers and goers, inspecting their papers, sending them on or turning them back, or laying hold, as their

capricious judgment deemed best for the dawning Republic.

(MONSIEUR DEFARGE and MADAME DEFARGE join the crowd as the scene shifts to the gates of Paris. The RESURRECTION MAN puts on his red cap, and the crowd waits expectantly as he inspects DARNAY's papers)

RESURRECTION MAN
(French accent) You are the emigrant Evremonde?

DARNAY
I am.

RESURRECTION MAN
Your age?

DARNAY
Twenty-seven.

RESURRECTION MAN
Married?

DARNAY
Yes.

RESURRECTION MAN
Where?

DARNAY
In England.

RESURRECTION MAN
Without doubt. Where is your wife, Evremonde?

DARNAY
In England.

RESURRECTION MAN
Without doubt. *(The RESURRECTION MAN*

hands DARNAY's papers to MONSIEUR DEFARGE) Emigrant Evremonde, you will follow me.

DARNAY
Where?

RESURRECTION MAN
You are consigned in secret to the prison at La Force.

DARNAY
Under what law? For what offense?

RESURRECTION MAN
We have new laws, and new offenses, since you were here last.

DARNAY
What is "in secret?" *(The RESURRECTION MAN does not answer)* I have come here voluntarily, in response to the written appeal of a fellow countryman. Is that not within my rights?

RESURRECTION MAN
Emigrants have no rights, Evremonde. *(MONSIEUR DEFARGE hands the papers back to the RESURRECTION MAN)* Merci, Citizen Defarge.

DARNAY
Defarge? Ernest Defarge? You keep a wine shop in the Quarter Saint Antoine, do you not?

MONSIEUR DEFARGE
I do.

DARNAY
I have heard of you. My wife came to your house to reclaim her father. Yes! Please Monsieur, all

here is so changed that I am absolutely lost. Will you render me a little help?

MONSIEUR DEFARGE
My duty is to my country and the People. I am the sworn servant of both. I can do nothing for you. Evremonde... Why would you come to France?

(MONSIEUR DEFARGE exits. The RESURRECTION MAN leads DARNAY off)

Scene Nineteen

(The scene shifts to the Manettes' home in London. Lucie and Miss Pross enter. Lucie is upset. Miss Pross has to work hard to keep up)

MISS PROSS
Miss Lucie! Miss Lucie! What on earth is wrong?

LUCIE
He has oppressed no man. He has imprisoned no man. Rather than harshly exacting payment of his dues, he relinquished them of his own free will. He left instructions to his steward to give the people what little there was to give. And for this service, he is to be imprisoned.

MISS PROSS
What are you talking about, Miss Lucie?

LUCIE
The decree.

MISS PROSS
What decree? There have been so many decrees

I've lost count.

LUCIE
They are arresting emigrants.

(The doorbell rings)

MISS PROSS
But you remember what Mister Carton said, how unreliable the news is from France during these troubled times.

LUCIE
I must go to him.

MISS PROSS
You what?

LUCIE
If I leave now, there is a chance I may overtake him before he arrives in Paris.
(CARTON enters)

MISS PROSS
Oh, Mister Carton! Thank goodness. Do talk some sense into her.

CARTON
I, Miss Pross? When have I ever been known to talk sense?

MISS PROSS
She's got it in her head to go to Paris!

CARTON
She... what? Lucie, you can't be serious.

LUCIE
I am quite serious. Charles would do no less if our positions were reversed.

CARTON
Charles would not have let you go to Paris in the first place.

LUCIE
Do you make a joke, sir?

CARTON
What? No, of course not.

LUCIE
You make it sound as if Charles had a choice.

CARTON
Didn't he?

LUCIE
You believe he would abandon the happiness of his chosen home, the life he has made for himself, the family he has begun, if he thought there was a choice? If he did so, then he would not be the man I chose for my husband.

CARTON
Lucie, please--

LUCIE
I did not give you leave to be so familiar! Why do you still come here? So many nights you have wandered here, moody and morose. When you care to talk, it is overshadowed by this cloud of caring for nothing. How weak you are in your misery.

MISS PROSS
Miss Lucie!

LUCIE
I fear he is not to be reclaimed. There is scarcely

a hope that anything in his character or fortunes is reparable now. *(CARTON is dumbstruck)* Miss Pross, I must ask you to take care of my father while I am gone.

MISS PROSS
I'm sorry, Miss Lucie, but I'm afraid I can't do that.

LUCIE
What? Why not?

MISS PROSS
I'm going with you.

LUCIE
I cannot ask that of you.

MISS PROSS
You cannot ask me not to. Since you were a small child I have been your shadow and protector, and there is no thing more important in my life. I shall endure any French tomfoolery to see my Ladybird safely home again.

LUCIE
But you have heard the danger--

MISS PROSS
The short and the long of it is that I am a subject of His Most Gracious Majesty King George the Third, and as such, my maxim is: Confound their politics, frustrate their knavish tricks, on him our hopes we fix, God save the King!

LUCIE
Miss Pross, I--

(DOCTOR MANETTE enters)

ACT TWO

DOCTOR MANETTE
Lucie, you needn't worry. I shall accompany you as well.

LUCIE
Are you certain, Father?

DOCTOR MANETTE
I am. Remember, I have been a prisoner of the Bastille. Such a reputation may serve as valuable currency under the new regime. *(LUCIE embraces DOCTOR MANETTE)* We shall find him, my dearest. Hold fast to that.

LUCIE
I must prepare. Miss Pross?

(LUCIE and MISS PROSS start to exit)

CARTON
Mrs. Darnay...

(LUCIE pauses. She does not turn back. She and MISS PROSS exit)

DOCTOR MANETTE
I believe you deserve more consideration and respect than was expressed to you this night, Mister Carton.

CARTON
Did she mean it, do you think?

DOCTOR MANETTE
Did she mean it? Yes, I think she did. But do you know why? *(CARTON shakes his head)* Because she is sure that you are capable of good things, gentle things, even magnanimous things. The only thing preventing it is yourself. Perhaps you

have seen the common shoemakers' bench kept here?

CARTON
I have.

DOCTOR MANETTE
I once yearned so frightfully for that occupation, and it was so welcome when it came. No doubt it relieved my pain much, by substituting the perplexity of the fingers for the perplexity of the brain. I have never been able to bear the thought of putting it quite out of reach. Even now the idea that I might need that former employment and not find it gives me a sudden sense of terror. But does not the retention of the thing involve the retention of the idea? If the thing were gone, might not the fear go with it?

CARTON
I do not understand.

DOCTOR MANETTE
I have a simple favor to ask you, regarding that shoemakers' bench.

CARTON
Anything.

DOCTOR MANETTE
When we are gone, get rid it for me.

(DOCTOR MANETTE exits as The RESURRECTION MAN enters)

RESURRECTION MAN
Sadly, sadly, the sun rose on no sadder sight than a man of good abilities and good emotions,

incapable of their directed exercise, incapable of his own help and his own happiness, sensible of the blight on him, and resigning himself to let it eat him away.

(CARTON exits)

Scene Twenty

(The RESURRECTION MAN dons his red cap as the scene shifts to the prison)

RESURRECTION MAN
For Charles Darnay it is not easy, with the face of his beloved wife fresh before him, to compose his mind to what it must bear. There was a turbulent and heated working of his heart that contended against resignation.

(DARNAY enters. He looks rough)

RESURRECTION MAN
(French accent) Ah, welcome at last, Monsieur! I apologize that you had to wait so long for your accommodations to be ready. The prison is always full to bursting, Evremonde. Fortunately some more room has been made available. Thirty-one today.

DARNAY
Thirty-one?

RESURRECTION MAN
A fine number. But it's early days yet. Wait here, Monsieur.

(The RESURRECTION MAN exits. The SEAMSTRESS enters from another direction. Her imprisonment has taken a toll on her appearance and her sanity)

SEAMSTRESS
Hello, Monsieur.

DARNAY
Hello.

SEAMSTRESS
It would be impertinent of me elsewhere, but may I ask your name and condition?

DARNAY
Charles Darnay. I am here... because that was not always my name. It was once Evremonde.

(The SEAMSTRESS recoils)

SEAMSTRESS
Evremonde? That name... is known to me.

DARNAY
I fear it is not a happy association. I have lived in England for many years. I came here because I hoped to set right some of my family's wrongs.

SEAMSTRESS
If you could have foreseen this, would you still have made the journey?

DARNAY
Troubled as the future was, it was still unknown, and in that ignorance lingers the shadow of hope.

How could such frightful deeds have a place in the conceptions of a gentle mind?

SEAMSTRESS
I hope you will not be here long, and that your term ends happily.

DARNAY
Thank you. But what brings you here?

SEAMSTRESS
"Plots." Though Heaven knows I am innocent of any. I was a seamstress. What plots could I lay?

DARNAY
Have you been here long?

SEAMSTRESS
Long enough. I shan't go home again.

DARNAY
Why do you say that?

SEAMSTRESS
I have no one to speak for me. My husband is gone. I have only a cousin, who lived far from me and would not have heard what has become of me. Those who knew me will be too afraid to come forward on my behalf. It is only a matter of time before my name is called and I am taken to the Conciergerie.

DARNAY
What happens there?

SEAMSTRESS
That is where the condemned spend their last days, until they are taken before Madame La Guillotine. Thirty-one today.

DARNAY
Thirty-one. *(The SEAMSTRESS starts to exit)* Wait! Please. When I was sentenced, the man told me I was to be held "in secret." Do you know what it means?

SEAMSTRESS
I am sorry for you, Monsieur.

DARNAY
Why?

SEAMSTRESS
No one will be told you are here. You may write letters, but no one will receive them. No one will come for you. They have buried you alive. I hope for your sake, Monsieur, that you have friends who love you, and who will know where to look for you.

(The RESURRECTION MAN enters, and gestures toward the exit)

RESURRECTION MAN
(French accent) This is yours, emigrant.

DARNAY
Am I to be kept apart from the others?

RESURRECTION MAN
Those are my instructions.

DARNAY
But this young woman is allowed the freedom of the prison.

RESURRECTION MAN
She is not held in secret, emigrant.

(DARNAY looks back to the SEAMSTRESS, who

lowers her head and exits. DARNAY exits into his cell)

RESURRECTION MAN
(Cockney accent) And here they left him, as if he were dead. Five paces by four and a half, five paces by four and a half, the prisoner walked to and fro in his cell, counting its measurement, and the roar of the city arose like muffled drums with a wild swell of voices added to them.

(The sound of a massive crowd cheering swells as the RESURRECTION MAN exits)

MONSIEUR DEFARGE
Liberty!

ALL
Liberty!

REVOLUTIONARY #1
Equality!

ALL
Equality!

REVOLUTIONARY #2
Fraternity!

ALL
Fraternity!

MADAME DEFARGE
Or Death!

ALL
Or Death!

(The sound of a falling blade silences the crowd. The crowd exits)

Scene Twenty-One

(The cheers continue as the scene shifts to a small apartment in Paris, where Lucie and Miss Pross are waiting. Their bags are still unpacked. Lucie is looking out a window)

LUCIE
What is that noise?

MISS PROSS
Miss Lucie! Your father told you to stay away from the windows.

LUCIE
Yes, but is it because he doesn't wish us to be seen, or he doesn't wish us to see what is happening in this dreadful city? *(DOCTOR MANETTE enters)* Father? Any news?

DOCTOR MANETTE
Your apprehensions were right, my dear. He was arrested the moment he arrived in Paris. He can send no messages to the outside world. If we had

not come, we might never have learned of his fate until it was too late.

LUCIE
How did you find him?

DOCTOR MANETTE
He is called before the tribunal today.

LUCIE
Today! Father, what can we do?

DOCTOR MANETTE
I have some hope that I may be able to do some good here. I have been a prisoner of the Bastille. There is no patriot in France who would not open their door to me. I believe I can rescue him from danger. It is a strange thing, though.

LUCIE
What?

DOCTOR MANETTE
You recall the man who looked after me before you found me? The wine shop owner?

LUCIE
Monsieur Defarge, yes.

DOCTOR MANETTE
It appears he has risen to a position of some prominence in the new regime. I believe he may be the one sitting in judgement at today's proceeding.

LUCIE
But surely he would be inclined to help you, wouldn't he?

DOCTOR MANETTE
If I recall correctly, it is not his good opinion we

should be courting.

LUCIE
Who's, then?

(There is a knock at the door)

DOCTOR MANETTE
Do not be frightened. As I have said, it appears I have a charmed life in Paris.

(He opens the door. MADAME DEFARGE enters)

MADAME DEFARGE
I received word that you had arrived in Paris. I wished to be sure I could identify you, for your safety. You are the wife of Evremonde?

LUCIE
I am Lucie Darnay. You are Madame Defarge, are you not?

MADAME DEFARGE
I am.

LUCIE
You are very welcome here. This is Miss Pross; she was my governess.

MISS PROSS
How do you do. *(MADAME DEFARGE ignores MISS PROSS completely, focused instead on scrutinizing LUCIE's face)* I'm sure I'm quite well, thank you!

LUCIE
Please, can you tell me if my husband is well?

MADAME DEFARGE
He was in good health, when last I saw him.

LUCIE
Bless you, Madame.

(LUCIE takes MADAME DEFARGE's hand and kisses it. "There was something in its touch that gave LUCIE a check.")

MADAME DEFARGE
I have seen what I came here to see. Good day.

LUCIE
Please be good to my poor husband. Please help me see him if you can.

MADAME DEFARGE
Your husband is not my business here.

LUCIE
For my sake, then, be merciful to him. I am more afraid of you than any of these others.

(For the first time, MADAME DEFARGE smile)

MADAME DEFARGE
Your father has much influence in Paris. I am certain his words will determine your husband's fate.

LUCIE
You have a husband yourself. What would you not do for him, in my place?

MADAME DEFARGE
We have borne this a long time. Is it likely the trouble of one poor wife would mean much to us now? You should hurry. The trial will begin soon.
(MADAME DEFARGE exits)

DOCTOR MANETTE
Courage, my dear Lucie. All goes well for us so far

– much better than it has for many poor souls here.

LUCIE
I know it. But that woman throws a shadow on me, and on all
my hopes.

DOCTOR MANETTE
Come my dear. We must hurry.

(They exit)

Scene Twenty-Two

(The scene shifts to the street outside the prison. LUCIE and DOCTOR MANETTE enter)

LUCIE
This is the prison?

DOCTOR MANETTE
My dear, there is an upper window there, where prisoners awaiting trial can be seen. Wait here. If I can, I will have Charles pass by so you may see each other. But be careful. It would be unsafe for you to make a sign of recognition. Wait for me here.

(DOCTOR MANETTE exits as the RESURRECTION MAN enters, wearing a red cap)

RESURRECTION MAN
(French accent) Good day, citizeness. *(LUCIE smiles in acknowledgement)* I say to you, good day, citizeness.

LUCIE
Bonjour.

RESURRECTION MAN
I have not seen you before, no? Walking here? It is a good spot. If you look up there, see? *(He points to some distant location. LUCIE looks)* Peeking above the wall? There she is! Our saint Guillotine! What do you think? Come here in the afternoon and you may watch her work. Forty times, just yesterday! Beautiful, is she not? Oh, but you have nothing to fear from her, citizeness! I can see that you are a patriot! Republic One and Indivisible! Liberty, Equality, Fraternity, or Death!

(Softly at first, as if from a distance, we hear a crowd of revolutionaries singing "La Carmagnole." As the crowd appears. The RESURRECTION MAN joins in the dance. It grows wilder and more violent as it continues, trapping LUCIE. She is tossed about by the swirling mob. The crowd passes through, leaving the RESURRECTION MAN and a terrified LUCIE in their wake)

LUCIE
What on earth was that?

RESURRECTION MAN
This was the Carmagnole, citizeness. That great song of the Revolution.

LUCIE
No battle could have been half so terrible as that dance.

RESURRECTION MAN
Next time you will dance it with us, no?

(The RESURRECTION MAN exits as DOCTOR MANETTE enters)

DOCTOR MANETTE
My dear! I heard the crowd. Are you all right?

LUCIE
Yes, Father. I just want to get away from this place.

(They exit)

Scene Twenty-Three

(The scene shifts to the tribunal. MONSIEUR DEFARGE acts as judge. MADAME DEFARGE stands off to the side, watching. The room is filled with REVOLUTIONARIES. The RESURRECTION MAN enters)

RESURRECTION MAN
Poor Charles Darnay stands accused, officially, of being an emigrant. And unofficially, of being an Evremonde. Either way, his life is forfeit to the Republic, under the decree which banishes all emigrants on pain of death. It is nothing that the decree was made after he returned to France. There he is, and there is the decree. He had been taken in France, and the People demand one thing.

ALL
Take off his head! He is the enemy! Long live the Republic! etc.

(MONSIEUR DEFARGE gavels the court to order)

MONSIEUR DEFARGE
Charles Evremonde, called Darnay, is it not true that you lived many years in England?

DARNAY
Undoubtedly, it is true.

MONSIEUR DEFARGE
Are you not an emigrant, then?

DARNAY
I voluntarily relinquished a title and station that was distasteful to me, and left my country to live by my own industry in England, rather than on the industry of the overladen people of France.

MONSIEUR DEFARGE
What proof have you of this?

DARNAY
I offer two witnesses: Thomas Gabelle, who was my steward, and my father in law, Doctor Alexandre Manette.

(An approving murmur runs through the crowd)

MONSIEUR DEFARGE
Why did you return to France when you did, and not sooner?

DARNAY
I had no means of living in France, save those I had resigned. In England, I live by giving instruction in the French language and literature. I returned on the pressing entreaty of a French citizen, whose life was endangered by my absence.

I came back to save a citizen's life, and bear testimony, at whatever personal hazard, to the truth. Is that criminal in the eyes of the Republic?

ALL
No! Set him free! Not guilty! etc.

MADAME DEFARGE
Husband!

(MONSIEUR DEFARGE *tries to gavel the court back to order again. During the noise,* MADAME DEFARGE *gives him a slip of paper. As* MONSIEUR DEFARGE *reads,* DOCTOR MANETTE *steps forward and gets* DARNAY's *attention*)

DOCTOR MANETTE
Charles! Charles!

DARNAY
Doctor Manette! My God, what are you doing here? Lucie is not with you, is she?

DOCTOR MANETTE
Of course she is. From the first hint of your troubles, nothing could keep her away.

DARNAY
You must go. You must get her out of France.

DOCTOR MANETTE
And so I shall, but we have no intention of leaving without you, my son.

(MONSIEUR DEFARGE *finishes reading*)

MONSIEUR DEFARGE
Is this true?

MADAME DEFARGE
It is, my husband.

MONSIEUR DEFARGE
Where did this come from?

MADAME DEFARGE
It was hidden in his cell.

MONSIEUR DEFARGE
Why did you not tell me of this before now?

MADAME DEFARGE
When I knit, do I take from the basket every tool and piece of yarn I might possibly use? Or do I take only what I know is needed at the time?

(Madame Defarge returns to her place with the crowd. Monsieur Defarge gavels the court back to order)

MONSIEUR DEFARGE
Charles Evremonde, called Darnay, you are to be returned to La Force. This tribunal will resume tomorrow.

DARNAY
Citizen, I demand to know how and why I am still a prisoner.

MONSIEUR DEFARGE
You have no right to question the decisions of this tribunal.

(DOCTOR MANETTE steps forward)

DOCTOR MANETTE
Do you know who I am?

MONSIEUR DEFARGE
Of course. We all know you, Citizen Doctor.

DOCTOR MANETTE
Will you answer my question, then? You have heard the people assembled here. Will you now set Charles Darnay free?

MONSIEUR DEFARGE
Citizen Doctor, not all the evidence has been presented.

DOCTOR MANETTE
What other evidence is there?

MONSIEUR DEFARGE
It appears a new accusation has been made against the prisoner.

DOCTOR MANETTE
Of what is he accused now?

MONSIEUR DEFARGE
Citizen Doctor, ask no more. If the Republic demands sacrifices from you, without doubt, you as a good patriot will make them. The Republic goes before all.

DOCTOR MANETTE
But at least tell us who has denounced him?

MONSIEUR DEFARGE
Do you ask that, Doctor?

DOCTOR MANETTE
I do.

MONSIEUR DEFARGE
Very well. Charles Evremonde, called Darnay, suspected enemy of the Republic, aristocrat, one of a family of tyrants, one of a race proscribed for using their abolished privileges to the infamous oppression of the people, you

have been denounced openly by a citizen of the Republic. Let your accuser step forward. *(There is a hush as the crowd waits to hear the name)* Doctor Alexandre Manette.

(The crowd erupts in shock)

DOCTOR MANETTE
Citizens, I protest to you that this is a forgery and a fraud! You know the accused to be the husband of my daughter. Those dear to her are dearer to me than my own life. Who and where is the false conspirator who says I denounce my own son?

(The crowd cries out in support of DOCTOR MANETTE; MADAME DEFARGE shouts over it)

MADAME DEFARGE
Nothing can be dearer to a true citizen than the Republic itself!

(The crowd hushes in fear of her)

MONSIEUR DEFARGE
Doctor Manette, when you were at the Bastille, you were confined in cell number one hundred and five, North Tower, is that correct?

DOCTOR MANETTE
It is.

MONSIEUR DEFARGE
I thought so. When you were under my care you knew yourself by no other name. Doctor Manette, when the tower fell, an examination was made of many of the cells, yours included. Hidden in a hole beneath a loose stone, a piece of paper was found. Here it is. Do you recognize

this, Doctor Manette?

(MONSIEUR DEFARGE hands the small, aged scrap of paper to DOCTOR MANETTE)

DOCTOR MANETTE
I do.

MONSIEUR DEFARGE
Is that your writing on it?

DOCTOR MANETTE
It is.

MONSIEUR DEFARGE
The note is dated the last month of the year Seventeen Hundred and Seventy-Five. You were a prisoner of the Bastille on that date, were you not?

DOCTOR MANETTE
I was.

MONSIEUR DEFARGE
The note says that ten years before, in December of 1765, a nobleman sought you out, requiring your medical expertise. You were taken in secret to a country house outside Paris. Is this correct?

DOCTOR MANETTE
It is.

MONSIEUR DEFARGE
Do you recall the nobleman's name?

DOCTOR MANETTE
Evremonde.

MONSIEUR DEFARGE
I'm sorry?

DOCTOR MANETTE
(Louder) Evremonde.

MONSIEUR DEFARGE
This Marquis St. Evremonde instructed you to care for two peasants, young woman and a younger man. The young man informed you that the nobleman had violated the woman and caused the deaths of the woman's husband and father. The young man came after the nobleman, who stabbed the young man, wounding him. Is this correct so far?

DOCTOR MANETTE
It is.

MONSIEUR DEFARGE
The young man died that night; the woman after a week in agony. The Marquis St. Evremonde then warned you to remain silent about the incident. Is that also correct?

DOCTOR MANETTE
Yes.

MONSIEUR DEFARGE
However, like a true citizen, you did not follow the command of the depraved Marquis. What, Citizen Manette, did you do?

DOCTOR MANETTE
I wrote a letter to the Court, reporting the incident.

MONSIEUR DEFARGE
And was Evremonde brought to justice?

DOCTOR MANETTE
No.

MONSIEUR DEFARGE
Tell us what happened.

DOCTOR MANETTE
That night, a man rang at my gate, demanding to see me. An urgent case in the Rue St. Honore, he said. There was a coach waiting.

MONSIEUR DEFARGE
But it did not take you to the Rue St. Honore, did it?

DOCTOR MANETTE
It took me to the Bastille. The Marquis was there. He had the letter I had written to the Court. He burned it in a lantern, before my eyes.

MONSIEUR DEFARGE
How long were you imprisoned in the Bastille?

DOCTOR MANETTE
Eighteen years.

MONSIEUR DEFARGE
Citizen Manette, please read the last passage of the note you wrote during your imprisonment.

DOCTOR MANETTE
But please, you must understand--

MONSIEUR DEFARGE
Just read your words, please.

DOCTOR MANETTE
This was written years ago, about another man entirely. You cannot possibly accept this as evidence--

MADAME DEFARGE
The people will decide what is and is not evidence,

Citizen.

MONSIEUR DEFARGE
Citizen Doctor, your letter. Please.

DOCTOR MANETTE
"If it had pleased God to put it in the hard heart of this man, in all these frightful years, to grant me any tidings of my dearest wife - so much as to let me know by a word whether alive or dead - I might have thought that God had not quite abandoned him. But now I believe the Marquis St. Evremonde has no part in His mercies. And he and his descendants, to the last of their race, I, Alexandre Manette, unhappy prisoner, do this last night of the year 1775, in my unbearable agony, denounce them to the times when all these things shall be answered for. I denounce them to Heaven and to earth."

(There is an uproar from the revolutionaries in the crowd)

MONSIEUR DEFARGE
Citizens of the Republic! Are you prepared to render a verdict?

ALL
Yes!

MONSIEUR DEFARGE
To the charge of being at heart and by descent an Aristocrat, an enemy of the Republic, and a notorious oppressor of the People, how do you find the prisoner?

ALL
Guilty!

MONSIEUR DEFARGE
Charles Evremonde, called Darnay, you are to be taken to the Conciergerie, there to await your sentence to be carried out no later than three o'clock tomorrow: Death, by guillotine!

(The crowd cheers as MONSIEUR DEFARGE bangs his gavel. He and MADAME DEFARGE exit. The revolutionaries drag DARNAY off as DOCTOR MANETTE holds LUCIE back as she tries to go after him)

LUCIE
Father! Do something! Save him!

(DOCTOR MANETTE takes LUCIE off)

Scene Twenty-Four

(The scene shifts to a marketplace. Miss Pross enters. Barsad enters, looking around to see if he's being observed. He sees Miss Pross and looks for a place to hide, but she spots him)

MISS PROSS
Solomon? Solomon, is that you?

(Unable to find anywhere to go, BARSAD turns to face MISS PROSS)

MISS PROSS
Oh Solomon! Dear Solomon! After not setting eyes upon you for so long, I find you here of all places?

BARSAD
Don't call me Solomon. Do you want to be the death of me?

MISS PROSS
My brother, have I ever been so hard with you that you ask me such a cruel question?

BARSAD
Then hold your tongue and come out of the street! Now, what do you want?

MISS PROSS
How dreadfully unkind of you to give me such a greeting, and show me no affection!

BARSAD
Do you think I'm surprised to see you? I knew you were here. I know of most people who are here. If you really don't want to endanger me, then go your ways as soon as possible, and let me go mine. I am on official business.

MISS PROSS
My brother Solomon, that had the makings in him of one of the best and greatest men in his native land of England, an official among foreigners. And such foreigners!

BARSAD
I knew it! You really are trying to kill me.

MISS PROSS
The gracious and merciful heavens forbid! How could you think that of me, Solomon?

BARSAD
That isn't my name! Not here.

MISS PROSS
What on earth do you mean? What should your name be, then?

(SYDNEY CARTON enters)

CARTON
John Barsad.

MISS PROSS
Why, Mister Carton! Is that you? What are you doing here?

CARTON
Don't be alarmed, Miss Pross. I was not far behind you on the road to Paris. I thought to present myself at a moment when I might be useful. I present myself here, to beg a few words with your brother.

MISS PROSS
But what business could you possibly have with him?

CARTON
I am sorry to tell you, Miss Pross, that your brother here is working for Mister Darnay's gaolers.

MISS PROSS
He couldn't be!

BARSAD
That's a damned lie.

CARTON
I remember faces, and yours is memorable enough. Knowing your previous association with Charles Darnay's misfortunes, I couldn't help but be curious after seeing you, of all people, coming out of the Conciergerie. So I followed you. It didn't take long to deduce your current occupation. I cannot help but feel that our paths have crossed again but for some great purpose.

BARSAD
What purpose?

Act Two

CARTON
Dear Miss Pross, may I suggest that you return to Doctor Manette's apartment? The Paris streets are not safe for good English women. There are unsavory characters about. And Miss Pross, may I prevail upon you to do one favor for me?

MISS PROSS
Of course.

CARTON
I would appreciate it if you would keep our meeting today a secret.

MISS PROSS
But why? Miss Lucie would be so relieved--

CARTON
Believe me, Miss Pross, it is safest for everyone if my presence in Paris remained unknown for a little while longer. Please do me this favor. I promise it shan't be long before you are repaid in full.

MISS PROSS
Bless you, Mister Carton. Solomon... I don't know what to say to you. You're not the man I thought you were.

(MISS PROSS exits)

CARTON
You're looking well for a dead man. What an excellent cover for a spy. What name are you using these days?

BARSAD
What do you want?

CARTON
I want answers. Darnay was on the verge of being acquitted, and then suddenly he is condemned. The judge, Defarge, went to a good deal of effort to find the evidence that could turn the crowd against him.

BARSAD
Defarge, or his wife.

CARTON
Why?

BARSAD
I wouldn't play at that game if I were you. You don't have the cards.

CARTON
You think not? I do have one ace I'm willing to play.

BARSAD
What's that?

CARTON
You, John Barsad. Look at you: I don't know what name you go by here, but you have made yourself a valued informer for the new Republican French government. But what would your new friends think if they found out their trusted agent was once in the pay of the French aristocracy?

BARSAD
They know all about it. They've chosen to overlook my past indiscretions and put my talents to use.

CARTON
Suppose I told the Committee you were still

working for them. Suppose I said you were still a spy for England? Suppose I said you were part of a cabal of Royalists conspiring to restore His Royal Majesty King Louis the Sixteenth to the throne?

BARSAD
That is preposterous. No one would believe you.

CARTON
Me? No, they wouldn't. But they might believe Doctor Alexandre Manette, Hero of the Bastille.

BARSAD
You wouldn't.

CARTON
Wouldn't I?

BARSAD
He would never lie under oath.

CARTON
You think so? Who knows what he did to survive eighteen years in that prison. What wouldn't he do to protect the ones he loves? The crowds adore him, you know. And you have seen how much influence the people have during these tribunals.

BARSAD
I'm no spy. Not anymore.

CARTON
You've been here long enough to know that you are whatever the mob thinks you are. I play my ace, Mister Barsad. Time to show your cards.

BARSAD
(Beaten) If they found out I helped you, the guillotine will be the least of my fears.

CARTON
Do what I say and there is a chance they won't find out. Thwart me, and I will denounce you this instant. I could not better testify my respect for your sister than by relieving her of her brother.

BARSAD
What do you want?

CARTON
You have access to the prison?

BARSAD
Yes.

CARTON
Then come with me.

(They exit)

Scene Twenty-Five

(The scene shifts to the Defarges' wine shop. MONSIEUR and MADAME DEFARGE enter. As they speak, the RESURRECTION MAN enters, but remains hidden from them)

MONSIEUR DEFARGE
I understand your wish, but one must stop somewhere, no? It's a question of when.

MADAME DEFARGE
We stop at extermination. She is an Evremonde by marriage. I see no reason why she should not also be added to the lists.

MONSIEUR DEFARGE
I can say nothing against it. But her father, the Doctor, has suffered much already. You saw him today, when his words were read. The anguish of his daughter must be dreadful to him.

MADAME DEFARGE
I have looked him in the face, and I have observed

that he is no true friend of the Republic.

MONSIEUR DEFARGE
You are not serious?

MADAME DEFARGE
The Doctor. His daughter. Add them to the lists. *(Pause)* You hesitate. You would see Evremonde rescued, even now!

MONSIEUR DEFARGE
No! Nothing of the sort. But I would leave the matter there. I say, stop there.

MADAME DEFARGE
You asked me once, why this family. Do you remember?

MONSIEUR DEFARGE
Of course.

MADAME DEFARGE
The family in the Doctor's papers, the peasant family destroyed by the Marquis St. Evremonde: That was my family. The young woman, cruelly used by those men, was my sister. The young man, dying of his wounds, was my brother. Those dead are my dead, and the summons to answer for those deeds falls to me.

MONSIEUR DEFARGE
My God, Therese.

MADAME DEFARGE
You understand now. The Doctor. His daughter. Twenty-five years I have waited for this day. Will you still tell me it is time to stop? Tell wind and fire when to stop, but never dare tell me! *(They exit)*

(BARSAD enters. He slips some coins to the RESURRECTION MAN, and they exit together)

Scene Twenty-Six

(The scene shifts to the apartment where DOCTOR MANETTE and LUCIE are staying. DOCTOR MANETTE and MISS PROSS sit in silence. CARTON enters)

CARTON
Doctor Manette?

DOCTOR MANETTE
Mister Carton? What are you doing here?

CARTON
Is Lucie here?

DOCTOR MANETTE
She is lying down. She is too distraught for guests now.

CARTON
No, I wanted to be sure she would not overhear us.

DOCTOR MANETTE
Miss Pross, would you--

MISS PROSS
I'll check on Miss Lucie.

(MISS PROSS exits, giving CARTON a look as she goes)

DOCTOR MANETTE
What is it?

CARTON
Doctor Manette, I know that I have never presented a figure that was worthy of your trust, but I must ask that you trust me now. You are in great danger. You and Miss Lucie. You are in danger of denunciation by Madame Defarge.

DOCTOR MANETTE
How do you know this?

CARTON
I have spoken to someone in whose best interest it is to keep me informed of such things. He has made your danger clear to me in sharp colors. But if you do exactly what I ask, I swear to you that no danger will follow you.

DOCTOR MANETTE
What would you ask of us?

CARTON
You must prepare to leave immediately. I will make arrangements to have a carriage here for you tomorrow to take you out of the city, and from thence to the coast. Be ready to travel by two o'clock tomorrow afternoon.

DOCTOR MANETTE
Lucie will not wish to leave while her husband is still alive.

CARTON
You must press upon her the danger of the situation, to yourself as well as to her. Tell her that her husband has arranged the transport, and that it was his last gift to her. Tell her whatever you need to tell her, but make sure she meets that carriage.

DOCTOR MANETTE
I'll see it done.

(CARTON takes a paper from his jacket)

CARTON
Once my seat in the carriage is occupied, would you give this to Lucie?

DOCTOR MANETTE
Surely you will be able to deliver it yourself.

CARTON
Please. I can trust no one else to deliver this. Not even myself.

DOCTOR MANETTE
(Taking the letter) When your seat is occupied.

CARTON
And then straight for England. Understand this: Change the course, or delay for any reason, and no life can possibly be saved.

DOCTOR MANETTE
I understand. I hope to do my part faithfully.

CARTON
And I mine. Goodbye, Doctor Manette.

(CARTON exits)

Scene Twenty-Seven

(The scene shifts to Darnay's cell. DARNAY is exhausted and terrified. A churchbell chimes two o'clock)

DARNAY
One hour left.

(The sound of a key turning a heavy lock. CARTON enters. After a moment, he takes DARNAY's hand)

CARTON
Of all people on this earth, you least expected to see me.

DARNAY
Are you a prisoner too?

CARTON
No. I come from your wife, dear Darnay. I bring a request from her. (*CARTON begins stripping off his clothes*) Change clothes with me.

DARNAY
I don't understand.

CARTON
There is no time. Put these on.

(Numb, DARNAY starts changing his clothes. CARTON takes Darnay's clothes and puts them on)

DARNAY
Carton, there is no escaping from this place. This is madness.

CARTON
It would be madness if I asked you to escape. If I asked you to do so, you would be right to refuse. Quickly, now.

DARNAY
It can't be done. Many have tried and have always failed. You will only add your death to mine.

CARTON
Hurry.

DARNAY
Do you have some sort of plan? What do you intend to do? *(CARTON does not answer. Looking at their clothing, realizing)* No. You cannot do this. I cannot live with such a thing on my conscience. You must--

CARTON
Wait! Someone is coming. Do you hear?

(DARNAY turns to the door, and CARTON hits DARNAY on the back of the head with a sap. DARNAY collapses, dazed)

CARTON
You out there! Come in!

(BARSAD enters. He stops when he sees the switch that has taken place)

BARSAD
The time is very short now... Evremonde.

CARTON
I know it well. My friend here, Mister Carton, has fainted. He is quite overwhelmed by our parting. You must take him to the carriage. In his pocket you will find the pass that allows him to leave the city. You will see, it bears his name and country.

BARSAD
Why are you doing this?

CARTON
Just tell Doctor Manette to remember our words from last night. Drive away and never look back. Go.

(BARSAD leads the groggy DARNAY out of the cell)

Scene Twenty-Eight

(The scene shifts to the street outside the Manettes' apartment. The RESURRECTION MAN enters)

RESURRECTION MAN
Fifty-two are to roll this afternoon on the life-tide of the city to the boundless everlasting sea. Before their cells are quit of them, new occupants are appointed. Before their blood runs into the blood spilled yesterday, the blood that is to mingle with theirs tomorrow is already set apart.

(MADAME DEFARGE enters, on her way to the Manette's. She stops and checks the pistol she carries with her before exiting)

RESURRECTION MAN (cont'd)
Madame Defarge has witnessed every one from the seat she keeps reserved.

(The RESURRECTION MAN exits as the scene shifts to Doctor Manette's apartment. MISS

PROSS is collecting the last of the Manettes' belongings when MADAME DEFARGE enters. The two women stare at each other for some time)

MADAME DEFARGE
The wife of Evremonde. Where is she?

MISS PROSS
You might, from your appearance, be the wife of Lucifer. Nevertheless, you shall not get the better of me. I am an Englishwoman.

MADAME DEFARGE
I wish to see her. I am come to make my compliments.

MISS PROSS
I know that your intentions are evil, and you may depend upon it, I'll hold my own against them.

MADAME DEFARGE
It will do her no good to keep herself concealed from me at this moment. Good patriots will know what this means. Let me see her.

MISS PROSS
No, you wicked woman. I am your match.

MADAME DEFARGE
Either tell her that I demand to see her, or stand out of the way.

MISS PROSS
I'll not leave a handful of that pretty hair upon your head, if you lay a finger on me!

MADAME DEFARGE
(Raising her voice) Citizen Doctor! Wife of Evremonde! Any person but this miserable fool, answer me! *(Pause)* There is no one here. Very

well. If they are fled, then they are guilty. They will be pursued and brought back.

MISS PROSS
You shall not leave here while I can hold you.

(MADAME DEFARGE *turns to leave. MISS PROSS charges with a war cry and tackles MADAME DEFARGE. The two women grapple on the floor until MADAME DEFARGE gains the upper hand. She separates herself from MISS PROSS for a moment and reaches for something hidden inside her clothing. MISS PROSS grabs a hold of MADAME DEFARGE and smashes her into furniture; MADAME DEFARGE fights her off by punching and clawing. They destroy the room in their battle. Finally MADAME DEFARGE manages to knock MISS PROSS momentarily senseless. MADAME DEFARGE, dazed herself, draws a gun and struggles to train it on MISS PROSS. MISS PROSS comes around and grabs the gun. The two women struggle over the weapon until it goes off with a loud bang. Both women freeze for a moment, staring at each other. At last, MADAME DEFARGE falls to the ground, dead. MISS PROSS is left holding the gun. The RESURRECTION MAN enters*)

MISS PROSS
Is there any noise?

RESURRECTION MAN
The usual noises, Miss Pross.

MISS PROSS
I don't hear you. What did you say?

RESURRECTION MAN
I say, the usual noises, Miss Pross.

Act Two   151

(The RESURRECTION MAN holds his hand out for the gun. MISS PROSS gives it to him)

MISS PROSS
Am I alive?

RESURRECTION MAN
You are indeed.

MISS PROSS
I don't hear anything.

(The sound of tumbrils in the street)

RESURRECTION MAN
Do you hear that? Those are the tumbrils, transporting the doomed of the day. Do you hear it, Miss Pross?

MISS PROSS
There was a great crash, and then a great stillness, and that stillness seems to be fixed and unchangeable, never to be broken any more as long as my life lasts.

RESURRECTION MAN
Come, Miss Pross. You cannot be late for the carriage. Miss Lucie is waiting for you.

(The RESURRECTION MAN helps MISS PROSS to her feet. She exits)

RESURRECTION MAN
(To audience) If she didn't hear the sound of those dreadful carts, it seemed unlikely that she would ever hear anything else in this world. And indeed, she never did.

(The RESURRECTION MAN exits)

Scene Twenty-Nine

(The scene shifts to the street. DOCTOR MANETTE and LUCIE enter)

LUCIE
Father, I don't understand. Why was Mister Carton in Paris?

DOCTOR MANETTE
I don't know, my dear. But he asked us to be here at this time, and I do believe he was in earnest. He gave me this to give to you.

(He hands LUCIE the letter. She takes it but does not read it yet)

LUCIE
I cannot go. I cannot leave until Charles...

DOCTOR MANETTE
We cannot stay, my love. It isn't safe for us. It isn't safe for anyone anymore. We must go as soon as--

(BARSAD enters, supporting a dazed DARNAY. DARNAY's head is covered)

BARSAD
Doctor Manette, is it?

DOCTOR MANETTE
It is.

BARSAD
I have Mister Carton here. He isn't well.

(DARNAY stumbles forward. LUCIE and DOCTOR MANETTE rush to support him. DARNAY's head gets uncovered)

LUCIE
Oh my God! Charles!

BARSAD
Carton. This is Sydney Carton. Here are his papers. *(BARSAD hands Carton's documents to DOCTOR MANETTE)* Now get in that carriage.

LUCIE
But what of...

BARSAD
Fifty-two are called before Madame Guillotine today, and fifty-two will answer. Now go.

(MISS PROSS enters. She and BARSAD see each other. BARSAD exits)

LUCIE
Sydney. Father, we cannot leave him like this! We cannot ask him--

DOCTOR MANETTE
He asks it of us! He makes this sacrifice for us! And now the only thing we can do for him is

ensure his sacrifice was not given in vain. Now you must help your husband to the carriage.

(The RESURRECTION MAN enters, wearing the red cap)

RESURRECTION MAN
(French accent) This carriage waits for you? Papers, please. *(DOCTOR MANETTE hands over several documents. The RESURRECTION MAN looks through them)* Alexandre Manette, French, physician.

DOCTOR MANETTE
I am he.

RESURRECTION MAN
Lucie Darnay, his daughter.

LUCIE
Yes.

RESURRECTION MAN
(Looking up from the papers) Darnay... wife of Evremonde?

LUCIE
I am.

RESURRECTION MAN
Hah! Evremonde is engaged elsewhere today, I understand. *(The next document)* Beatrice Pross, English, governess. *(MISS PROSS realizes he is talking to her, and nods. The RESURRECTION MAN moves on to the last document)* Sydney Carton, English, advocate. *(The RESURRECTION MAN eyes DARNAY closely)* Is he unwell?

DOCTOR MANETTE
He is not in strong health, and has just said fare-

well to a friend who is under the displeasure of the Republic.

RESURRECTION MAN
That's not such a big deal. Many enough are under the displeasure of the Republic. *(He hands the papers back)* Your papers, sir.

DOCTOR MANETTE
May we depart, citizen?

RESURRECTION MAN
You may depart. *(The group begins a hasty exit)* Wait! *(They freeze)*

DOCTOR MANETTE
What is it?

RESURRECTION MAN
How many today?

DOCTOR MANETTE
I don't understand you.

RESURRECTION MAN
To the guillotine. How many today? Have you heard?

DOCTOR MANETTE
Fifty-two.

RESURRECTION MAN
Ah. I thought so. A brave number. I love it. *(Pause)* Bon voyage.

(The group exits. Lights shift to LUCIE, who opens Carton's letter. CARTON enters separately)

CARTON
(Narrating the letter) My dearest Lucie, do not grieve. I promised you once that I would do

anything for you, and for any who were dear to you. Grieve for France, grieve for those who cannot see the future in the past, but do not grieve for me.

Scene Thirty

(The scene shifts to reveal CARTON in the prison. The sounds of a crowd outside. The SEAMSTRESS enters, led in by the RESURRECTION MAN)

SEAMSTRESS
Citizen Evremonde? I entertained the hope that you had been released. *(Carton shakes his head)* I'm sorry to hear it. *(Pause)* I've done nothing. The Republic is to do much good for us poor, and I'm willing to die if the Republic will profit from my death, but I do not know how that can be. Do you? *(Pause)* I am just a seamstress, Citizen Evremonde, and far beneath your station. I am not afraid. But... will you let me hold your hand?

CARTON
Of course.

(CARTON holds his hand out. Something in his voice makes the SEAMSTRESS pause. She gets a good look at his face)

SEAMSTRESS
Who...? *(Pause)* Are you dying for him?

CARTON
And his family. Yes.

(She takes his hand. They face forward. The sound of the guillotine crashing down, and the crowd cheers)

SEAMSTRESS
May I ask you a question?

CARTON
Yes.

SEAMSTRESS
I have a cousin, my only relative, an orphan like myself, whom I love dearly. Poverty parted us, and she knows nothing of my fate. Do you think... Do you think that it will seem long to me, while I wait for her?

CARTON
It cannot be. There is no time where we are going, and no trouble either.

(The guillotine crashes again, and the crowd cheers again. The RESURRECTION MAN enters)

SEAMSTRESS
Is the moment come? *(CARTON nods)*

CARTON
"I am the Resurrection and the Life, saith the Lord: he that believeth in me, though he were dead, yet shall he live: and whosoever liveth and believeth in me shall never die."

(The SEAMSTRESS kisses CARTON.

The RESURRECTION MAN *leads the* SEAMSTRESS *off.* LUCIE *continues reading the letter)*

CARTON
I see the long ranks of new oppressors who have risen on the destruction of the old, perishing by this retributive instrument, before it shall cease out of its present use. I see a beautiful city and a brilliant people rising from this abyss, and, in their struggles to be truly free, in their triumphs and defeats, through the long years to come, I see the evil of this time gradually making expiation for itself and wearing out.

(The sound of the guillotine crashes again. The RESURRECTION MAN *re-enters.* CARTON *starts to walk toward him when* MONSIEUR DEFARGE *enters)*

MONSIEUR DEFARGE
Wait. *(*CARTON *freezes, careful not to turn and let* MONSIEUR DEFARGE *see his face)* Gaoler, Citizeness Defarge is not yet come, and she... has a special interest in witnessing the passing of this prisoner's sentence.

RESURRECTION MAN
(French accent) If she has not come by now, I am afraid she will miss it. I cannot vary from the lists.

MONSIEUR DEFARGE
She has never missed before. Her chair is empty, waiting for her.

RESURRECTION MAN
Bad fortune, Citizen.

MONSIEUR DEFARGE
Therese! Has anyone seen her? Therese Defarge!

(MONSIEUR DEFARGE exits, calling for his wife. DARNAY enters and joins LUCIE, who continues reading)

CARTON
(Narrating the letter) I see the lives for which I lay down mine, peaceful, useful, prosperous and happy. I see Her with a child upon her bosom, who bears my name. I see her father, aged and bent, but otherwise restored, and faithful to all men in his healing office, and at peace. I see her and her husband, their course done, lying side by side in their last earthly bed, and I know that each was not more honored and held sacred in the other's soul, than I was in the souls of both. I see their child, who bears my name, grown into a man. I see him, foremost of just judges and honored men, bringing a boy of his own to this place, then fair to look upon, with not a trace of this day's disfigurement, and I hear him tell the child this story.

(The RESURRECTION MAN takes off his red cap)

RESURRECTION MAN
They said of him, about the city that night, that it was the peacefullest man's face ever beheld there. Many added that he looked sublime and prophetic.

CARTON
(Narrating the letter) It is a far, far better thing that I do, than I have ever done; it is a far, far better rest that I go to, than I have ever known.

RESURRECTION MAN
Good night.

(Blackout)

END OF PLAY

ABOUT THE AUTHOR

British novelist Charles Dickens was born on February 7, 1812, in Portsmouth, England. His father was a clerk in the Naval Pay Office and when young Charles was 12 years old, his father was imprisoned for debt and Charles was put to work in a blacking factory. At fifteen he found work as an office boy to an attorney, and two years later he became a freelance reporter. He published his first short story in 1833, under the psydonym 'Boz'.

Over the course of his writing career, he wrote the beloved classic novels THE PICKWICK PAPERS, OLIVER TWIST, THE OLD CURIOSITY SHOP, BARNABY RUDGE, A CHRISTMAS CAROL, LITTLE DORRIT, BLEAK HOUSE, NICHOLAS NICKLEBY, DAVID COPPERFIELD, GREAT EXPECTATIONS, and A TALE OF TWO CITIES.

On June 9, 1870, Dickens died of a stroke in Kent, England, leaving his final novel, THE MYSTERY OF EDWIN DROOD, unfinished.

ABOUT THE PLAYWRIGHT

Christopher M. Walsh is a writer and actor whose work has been produced in the U.S. and Canada. In 2014 he was nominated for a Non-Equity Joseph Jefferson (Jeff) Award for his adaptation of Charles Dickens' A Tale of Two Cities. Other adaptations include THE COUNT OF MONTE CRISTO by Alexandre Dumas, THE CITY & THE CITY by China Miéville, and SOON I WILL BE INVINCIBLE by Austin Grossman. Christopher is also a two-time finalist in the Deathscribe Festival of Horror Radio Plays, produced by Chicago's WildClaw Theatre, winning the coveted Bloody Axe award for FRACTURE ZONE.

As an actor, Christopher has performed with a number of companies in and around the Chicago area. He is a proud member of the artistic ensemble at Lifeline Theatre, based in Chicago's Rogers Park neighborhood. Lifeline specializes in stage adaptations of literary works.

Originally from Muskegon, MI, he moved to Chicago in 1994 to study acting at Columbia College. He lives in Chicago with his wife and two cats. Follow his adventures online at christophermwalsh.com.

ABOUT LIFELINE THEATRE

Lifeline Theatre is driven by a passion for story. The ensemble process supports writers in the development of literary adaptations and new work, while their theatrical and educational programs foster a lifelong engagement with literature and the arts. A cultural anchor of the Rogers Park neighborhood in Chicago, they are committed to deepening their connection to an ever-growing family of artists and audiences, both near and far.

Lifeline Theatre's history of extraordinary world premiere adaptations includes MainStage productions of PRIDE & PREJUDICE, THE OVERCOAT, THE LEFT HAND OF DARKNESS, THE TALISMAN RING, JANE EYRE, CAT'S CRADLE, AROUND THE WORLD IN 80 DAYS, THE KILLER ANGELS, A ROOM WITH A VIEW, THE ISLAND OF DR. MOREAU, THE MARK OF ZORRO, MARIETTE IN ECSTASY, NEVERWHERE, THE MOONSTONE, WATERSHIP DOWN, and THE COUNT OF MONTE CRISTO.

Lifeline also produced world premiere adaptations of J. R. R. Tolkein's THE LORD OF THE RINGS trilogy (THE FELLOWSHIP OF THE RING, THE TWO TOWERS, AND THE RETURN OF THE RING) and four installments of the Dorothy L. Sayers Lord Peter Wimsey mysteries (WHOSE BODY?, STRONG POISON, GAUDY NIGHT, and BUSMAN'S HONEYMOON).

Family MainStage productions have included A WRINKLE IN TIME, LIZARD MUSIC, THE SNARKOUT BOYS AND THE AVACADO OF DEATH, THE PHANTOM TOLLBOOTH, JOURNEY OF THE SPARROWS, THE SILVER CHAIR, JOHNNY TREMAIN, and TREASURE ISLAND.

In 1986 Lifeline inaugurated its KidSeries program. Productions have included MR. POPPER'S PENGUINS, MIKE MULLIGAN AND HIS STEAM SHOVEL, BUNNICULA, JAMES AND THE GIANT PEACH, THE STORY OF FERDINAND, MRS. PIGGLE-WIGGLE, MY FATHER'S DRAGON, CLICK CLACK MOO: COWS THAT TYPE, THE STINKY CHEESE MAN, DUCK FOR PRESIDENT, THE TRUE STORY OF THE 3 LITTLE PIGS!, THE VELVETEEN RABBIT, THE LAST OF THE DRAGONS, and ARNIE THE DOUGHNUT.

Plays commissioned by Lifeline Theatre have gone on to publication, numerous regional and national tours, and to more than a hundred subsequent productions across over forty U.S. states, five Canadian provinces, as well as in England and Ireland.

FOR MORE INFORMATION
VISIT WWW.LIFELINETHEATRE.COM

lifeline
THEATRE
Big Stories, Up Close

Other Plays From SORDELET INK

The Count of Monte Cristo
by Christoper M Walsh
adapted from the novel by Alexandre Dumas

The Moonstone
by Robert Kauzlaric
adapted from the novel by Wilkie Collins

The Woman in White
by Robert Kauzlaric
adapted from the novel by Wilkie Collins

Season on the Line
by Shawn Pfautsch
adapted from Herman Melville's Moby-Dick

Hatfield & McCoy
by Shawn Pfautsch

It Came From Mars
by Joseph Zettelmaier

The Gravedigger
by Joseph Zettelmaier

Ebenezer - a Christmas Play
by Joseph Zettelmaier

Once A Ponzi Time
by Joe Foust

Eve of Ides
by David Blixt

Made in the USA
Lexington, KY
01 December 2016